Wye Valley

40 Hill and Riverside Walks

The author and publisher have made every effort to ensure that the information in this publication is accurate, and accept no responsibility whatsoever for any loss, injury or inconvenience experienced by any person or persons whilst using this book.

published by
pocket mountains ltd
6 Church Wynd, Bo'ness EH51 0AN
pocketmountains.com

ISBN: 978-1-9070250-1-3

Text copyright © Ben Giles 2009
Photography copyright © Ben Giles 2009

The right of Ben Giles to be identified as the Author of this work has been asserted by him in accordance with the Copyright, Designs and Patents Act 1988

A catalogue record for this book is available from the British Library

Printed in Poland

Introduction

Since 1971 the Wye Valley has been designated an Area of Outstanding Natural Beauty (AONB), covering on average an 8km wide corridor from just south of Hereford in the north to Chepstow in the south. The lower Wye Valley, which has the AONB as its core, divides the lowlands of southern England and the uplands of South Wales, and incorporates significant parts of three counties, Herefordshire, Gloucestershire, and Monmouthshire. From the broad riverside meadows of the Herefordshire plain to the soaring limestone cliffs of the lower gorge near Chepstow, from the industrial heritage of the Forest of Dean in the east to the far-reaching views of the Trellech plateau in the west, the landscape of the lower Wye Valley can claim to be one of the most varied and picturesque places in Britain to explore on foot.

The Wye Valley has long claimed to be the birthplace of British tourism. At the end of the 18th century, tourists in search of the picturesque came to experience the dramatic river scenery on a two-day boat trip form Ross to Chepstow, in what became known as the Wye Tour. At the same time, it was also an industrial centre producing iron ore, coal, wire, paper, bark for tanning, and timber for the building of ships and cathedrals. In this connection the Forest of Dean has looked both east to the Severn and west to the Wye. The flotilla of boat tours and the spoils of the industrial age may have long since faded,

but their effects and influence have not been completely effaced. One of the joys of walking in an area with such a rich past is stumbling across the remains and reminders of past inhabitants and the lives they led.

About this guide

This guide contains forty circular routes, covering an area somewhat broader than the AONB but within similar north-south boundaries. This collection of walks is split into five areas: Hereford Lowlands and the Woolhope Dome; Archenfield and the Monnow and Trothy Valleys; The Wye Gorge; The Forest of Dean; The Trellech to Chepstow Plateau. In part, the areas reflect the diverse geology and ecology of the landscape, but they are in no way essentially distinct or separate. Each has its own particular attractions and character, but there is much that is shared between all five areas.

Most of the routes are intended as comfortable walks or strolls, manageable by all willing to put one foot in front of another, at most requiring half a day to complete. Occasionally, the cumulative ascent may leave unseasoned legs a little stiffer, but in general the walking is on well-worn paths, lanes and tracks, which should require minimal time and effort for route-finding. However, the sketch maps serve an illustrative purpose and it is recommended that the relevant OS 1:25,000 map is carried – just two are needed to cover all areas (OS Explorers OL14 and 189), both of which are readily available in local shops. For those who enjoy full day walks, some routes can readily be lengthened, while others can be combined for a longer excursion. The recommended time given for each walk is an estimate based on average walking speed, with an allowance added in for ascent and the type of ground. This will vary significantly, with individual ability and preference as well as the seasonal effects on conditions underfoot – especially across fields. It is hoped that there is plenty of interest along the routes themselves and it would be very possible to spread a short walk over a half day; conversely, most routes are short enough to attempt two in a day.

Getting around and accommodation

The main towns of the lower Wye Valley are Hereford, Ross-on-Wye, Monmouth and Chepstow. All are on regular bus routes, while train stations are located at Hereford and Chepstow. An effort has been made to include walks which can be reached by using local bus services. However, many of the outlying rural areas are only intermittently served on both a weekly and seasonal basis. Further information is available from the tourist information centres in the towns listed above and from Traveline. Parking in small villages and hamlets can be a sensitive issue, but there are often areas designated for visitors. Pubs and inns are usually very accommodating, especially if the intention is to visit before or after a walk. Cycling is becoming increasingly popular in the area, and it would be feasible to combine the two activities, especially in the Forest of Dean which has an extensive network of cycle tracks. For accommodation, the area is well served by hotels, guesthouses and B&Bs, both in towns and villages and also in the surrounding countryside. In addition, there are campsites, youth hostels and even wigwams available.

Access and dogs

The Wye Valley is an area of mixed farming, with arable, dairy and sheep farming all present. At lambing time, farmers request that dogs are kept on leads. The presence of dogs for cows with calves can be problematic and it is not unheard of for cattle to behave in a very protective way. Even without a dog, cows which have recently calved should be left well alone. If in doubt, it is usually advisable and possible to find a short detour to avoid livestock. Most paths covered in the routes are well used and well maintained by various agencies, but in spring and summer hedges and undergrowth grow vigorously and nettles and brambles can infiltrate narrower paths and stile crossings.

A perspective on the landscape

To a Neolithic farmer, pausing at the end of a day on the steep slopes above the gorge of the, as yet unnamed, River Wye some 5000 years ago, the view westwards would have been filled with the sight of a rolling plateau of wooded hills, marked here and there by the rising smoke from wood fires, and framed on the horizon by the silhouetted shadows of black mountains. He might well have shuddered at venturing into the valley below and braving its waters wandering beneath towering cliffs. More likely he would have preferred to head southeast over a more thickly-wooded plateau on well-worn trackways to the salty waters of the large estuary to trade his surplus food for pottery and flints and luxuries. On returning, should he suddenly have found himself in the 21st century, what might have caught his immediate attention is the probable increase in tree cover on the slopes of the valley below. True, above there would be more clearings and fields; perhaps he would nod in agreement with Wordsworth's appreciation of 'lines of Sportive wood run wild'. The rumblings from the valley of commuter and daytripper traffic and the chainsaws of the Forestry Commission would have been unidentifiable to him, but so too would they have been to the Wye tourists of the 18th century – the road was only constructed in 1824, in places still requiring continual efforts to keep it from sliding into the river, and many woods were then still managed by coppicing. The towers and spires of churches and the unnatural lines of quarrying would perhaps have arrested his eye and the transformation of trackways into tarmac would have felt strange underfoot. But he would have been as puzzled and inquisitive as any modern walker on discovering mile after mile of moss-covered drystone walls or the crumbled remains of a charcoal-burner's or miner's cottage now invaded by roots and creepers, let alone the rusting remains of iron bridges extending to tunnelled openings in the hillside or the arresting sight of so many dwellings, and what dwellings, gathered together on the floodplains of the river. And what to make of the thundering tide on the A40's dual carriageways? And yet he might, just, despite the millennia of difference and change, have managed an amazed but quizzical smile on seeing that the line of the landscape was still, in essence, recognisable.

Below Hereford the River Wye turns south towards the market town of Ross, on its way executing a series of increasingly flamboyant meanders. The banks of the river are dotted with small settlements and villages, and with just a handful of roadbridges along the whole stretch there is still a great sense of rural seclusion. The floodplain here is generally broad and surrounded by a series of lowland hills; in places such as Ballingham, How Caple and Ross these wooded slopes rise steeply above the river, at times exposing the underlying rock of old red sandstone. Not least is the more substantial area of hills to the east, the Woolhope Dome, rising sharply to over 250m above the villages of Mordiford and Fownhope. Of geological and botanical importance, the Dome has drawn naturalists and geologists from all over the world.

Old lych gate at Woolhope ▶

Herefordshire Lowlands and the Woolhope Dome

The Mordiford loop

Distance **7km** Time **2-3 hours**
Terrain **fields and woodland paths**
Map **OS Explorer 189** Access **bus (453)
from Hereford**

**From the riverside village of Mordiford
climb up into the rolling limestone
country of the Woolhope Dome, an area
famous for its varied natural history,
before meandering back along the pretty
Pentaloe Brook.**

The bridge at Mordiford dates back to
the 14th century and is one of the oldest
bridges in Herefordshire. Before then the
crossing of the River Lugg was by way of
an ancient ford. A little above the bridge is
the confluence of the River Frome, and a
few hundred metres below the Lugg joins
the Wye. From the bridge the impressive
red-brick rectory can be seen and nearby is
the church, dedicated to the Holy Rood,
which dates in origin from Norman times
and contains a Record of Occurrence of

27th May 1811, recording the details of a
catastrophic flood of the Pentaloe
Brook, which flows into the Lugg just
below the bridge.

At the far end of the village, near the
Moon Inn, where parking is available with
permission, a minor road leads east
towards Haugh Wood and Woolhope.
After 200m take the signed footpath on
the left uphill through woodland, out into
fields and on to the top of the hill. From
here a grassy track takes you northwards
on top of a broad ridge with wonderful
views of Backbury Hill.

In the woodland ahead, a right turn
leads to a lane and a little way along it a
bridleway strikes up Backbury Hill, once
the site of an Iron Age hill fort though now
covered in woodland and gorse. The path
soon levels out and contours round the
south side of the hill before descending to
Broomy Green and a junction with a
forestry track into a conifer plantation.

◀ Ruined timber-framed cottage above Pentaloe Brook

Here, dog-leg right and then left at the first house down over fields with stunning views ahead. At the lane a left turn leads to the hamlet of Checkley and the Pentaloe Brook. A path now heads southwest over a series of fields, with the brook never far away on the left, and then enters Bears Wood, so called as it is reputedly where the last brown bear was killed in Herefordshire. The route is often muddy here and soon crosses the stream at a bridge, but it may not be worth washing the mud off yet!

Continue by the brook and at a clearing bear right. The brook soon bends away from the path; after 150m look out for the signed path which leads right out of the woodland into a field, down past a derelict timber-framed house to a field-edge track and the brook. There is a legend that a Wyevern, a green dragon, used to descend from the woods above the village to devour livestock and people. In one version the dragon was befriended by a little girl, but the alarmed villagers persuaded a condemned criminal to try to kill the dragon in return for a pardon. Hiding in a cider barrel where the dragon came down to the river to drink, he shot it with an arrow, but the dragon had its revenge while still alive by incinerating the condemned man with its last breath.

Bear left with the brook and soon the houses of Pentaloe Close appear ahead. Aim diagonally right across the field to the edge of the housing and follow the waymarks through the estate to the road. Here, turn right to return to Mordiford.

Woolhope and Marcle Hill

Distance 10km **Time** 3 hours
Terrain undulating fields and lanes
Map OS Explorer 189 **Access** bus (453)
from Hereford

Explore the rolling countryside at the heart of the Woolhope Dome and experience views at their best from the ridge along Marcle Hill.

Woolhope is located to the southeast of Hereford in the middle of steep-sided hills known as the Woolhope Dome, an area with a unique geological background. It also gave its name to The Woolhope Club. Founded in 1851 as the Woolhope Naturalists' Field Club, its interests now cover the local history, archaeology, and architecture of Herefordshire, as well as natural history and geology; its headquarters and Club Library are in the Woolhope Room in Hereford Library. The walk starts from the centre of Woolhope by the lych gate to the church and the Crown Inn, where there is parking with permission.

Walk eastwards out of the village, towards Putley, down the hill with views of Marcle Hill ahead, passing Court Farm, and take the first lane on the right just before the Butcher's Arms pub, a black and white timbered house. Where the lane bends left, keep on uphill through Beans Butts Wood, past buildings to a field above. From the top of the field there are extensive views back to the Black Mountains and into Mid Wales. Here, the underlying rock of Silurian limestone, some 400 million years old, contrasts with the old red sandstone found in much of the nearby Wye river valley and gives rise to the paler soils underfoot as well as the variety of woodland, wildflower meadows and extensive hedgerows.

Cross into Busland Wood, an ancient woodland full of bluebells in spring, and descend to a field and across a dry valley up to the road at Hooper's Oak. Turn right along the ridge, which has been in use as

◄ Cascades near Whittlebury Farm

a travellers' route since at least the Bronze Age. There are extensive views northeastwards to the Malvern Hills and southeastwards to the Cotswolds. Where the road bends left at a junction, take the path ahead up steps (just down from the junction is a picnic area and car park with a useful display board about the local geology). Continue along the ridge on a field-edge path for 2km, passing the high point of the ridge and then descending past a mast.

On reaching a delightful sunken trackway, turn right along the edge of Lyndalls Wood, downhill to where the track becomes a lane and soon after crosses a stream. Just round the left bend, take a path off right across fields to Whittlebury Farm, with its pretty stream and orchards. Cross the road and over two more fields with the stream nearby on the left, passing another Court Farm, a 15th-century manor house with interesting ornamental chimney stacks, to the tranquil church of Sollers Hope beyond. The current church dates from the 14th century, itself the restoration of a Saxon building, and was financed by the brother of Dick Whittington, the famous Mayor of London.

Leave the churchyard by the west gate and turn right across horse paddocks past the tump, a mound which is the remains of a Romano-British camp. Bear left with the stream and then up across fields to a gap between the alder-lined stream on the left and Long Wood on the right. Cross the stream and go over the brow of the hill to a stile, with views ahead to Woolhope. Here, turn left and soon cross a footbridge before bearing right into the adjacent field. Now make for the house ahead and onto a lane which passes Alford's Mill, a former cider mill. Wander along this pleasant lane, bearing left at a T-junction, for just over 1km back to Woolhope.

Holme Lacy riverside wander

Distance 8km **Time** 2 hours
Terrain riverside paths and parkland
Map OS Explorer 189 **Access** bus (454)
from Hereford

Stroll along the sweeping meanders of the River Wye to a lost medieval village and through the grounds of one of the largest and oldest country houses in Herefordshire.

At the western edge of the village, the B4399 passes over the old Ross to Hereford railway line. From the bridge, where there is room for a few cars, you can look down into the deep cutting – enthusiasts can descend a short path and explore it – but the walk follows the signed field-path above the railway cutting northwards towards the River Wye and round the top of the field to the right. Depending on the season the river can be glimpsed through the trees at the bottom of the steep slope. The lower path at the river's edge has long been overgrown and

eroded, an indication of the powerful meandering nature of the Wye below Hereford. Cross three more fields before descending through a small copse to the riverside.

The route now follows the river round its long meander. At the bend's apex the River Lugg slips with barely a murmur into the waters of the Wye and here the riverside meadows now stand empty, except for grazing livestock. Once, however, they would have been populated by people known as 'brinkers', property owners who fiercely defended their rights to fish the 'free waters' of the Wye and claim a valuable addition to their diet. Further on is Holme Lacy Bridge, whose forerunner used to be adorned by some substantial spiked iron railings – an incentive to stop and pay the toll to cross the river; and for vehicles it is still one of only three crossing points over the Wye between Hereford and Ross.

Cross the road and continue by the river

◄ The River Wye near Holme Lacy

for 1.5km in the same direction round the next left bend to a lane, called Church Road. Here you can see low mounds and earthworks which may indicate the remains of a sizeable medieval village, with the church of St Cuthbert now standing isolated, surrounded by riverside meadows which are susceptible to flooding. It can be an eerie place, but a short detour left leads to the splendid church with its effigies of the Scudamore family inside. Here, a detailed guidebook is available, produced by The Churches Conservation Trust.

Westwards along Church Road at the bend the route passes through some cowgates over the line of the disused railway and in the middle of the far side of the field crosses onto a road. A dog-leg left past the Old Schoolhouse and then right takes you into a pretty orchard. At its top right corner is the parkland of Holme Lacy House, now a hotel but for much of the last century it was used as a mental hospital. Before then it had been one of the seats of the Scudamore family, who now reside at Kentchurch Court near

Grosmont. In fact, in the late 17th century the Scudamores had themselves pulled down an existing brick house, built in the reign of Henry III by the Lacy family who had originally come over to England with William the Conqueror. As you now pass the lake there is a sweeping view up to the house.

At the top of the field, turn right onto a lane, past the delightful walled gardens and lodges of the house and parkland, back to the B4399 and Holme Lacy. Turn right here to reach the railway bridge.

Fownhope and Capler Camp

Distance 8km **Time** 2-3 hours
Terrain riverside and field paths,
woodland, steep slopes around Capler
Camp **Map** OS Explorer 189 **Access** bus
(453) from Hereford

**A leisurely approach along the river, then
a climb up to the lofty ramparts of Capler
Camp, gives some of the most varied
walking in this part of the Wye Valley.**

Fownhope is an attractive village on the
east bank of the River Wye and is worth
exploring in its own right, not least if you
happen to be visiting on Oak Apple Day at
the start of June when a parade to
celebrate Charles II's triumphant entry
into London in 1660 finishes at the black
and white timbered Green Man Inn, which
has been a coaching inn and courthouse
since the 15th century. The walk starts
opposite the fire station and the road to
Woolhope.

Ferry Lane leads down to the River Wye
and serves as a reminder that the village

was once an important port between
Hereford and Ross. Barges used to carry
bark for use in the tanning industry
downstream to Lydbrook, where they
would be reloaded with a return cargo of
coal. Beyond Ferry Boat Cottage, bear left
into fields and head south to reach the left
bank of the Wye and on to Leabrink
House, sited in a picturesque position on a
bend in the river where fishing is popular.

The route now heads up over the
shoulder of the hill, with views opening
out to the south and west, to reach a
stone barn before descending right to the
floodplain once more. Bear left over fields
to reach Mancell's Ferry, with views across
the river to Ballingham Hill. Here was a
popular crossing point, supervised at one
time by a Mr Mancell who gave his name
to the cottage. When the water is low
enough, the former landing stages are
clearly visible under the opposite bank
and it is still a good place for a picnic.

The riverside path continues beyond the

◄ Old water pump at Fownhope

cottage and ahead is Capler Camp hill fort hidden in the trees. After 1km, reach Capler Wood and turn left uphill to reach the road, then right up to the viewpoint, with the trees providing welcome shade on a hot summer's day. Now the route turns northwards to pick up the Wye Valley Walk uphill and round the south side of Capler Camp, passing between the prominent earth ramparts to reach the stone buildings on its eastern edge. This is another Iron Age hill fort, one of many in the area, and it is superbly positioned to survey the low ground to the north, though there is now extensive tree cover. Ignore the track off right to the triangulation point and follow the Wye Valley Walk steeply down the north side of the hill to Caplor Farm.

Here the route leaves the Wye Valley Walk and heads in a northwesterly direction over fields, along a right of way which starts at the back of the buildings at the lower end of the farm. Aim for the left of a pair of gates and a man-made lake before following the small stream for 200m.

The route dog-legs left, then right before heading over the rise and down to a footbridge over a stream and up to the walled garden of derelict Nash Farm. In the far left corner of this field, cross a stile and in 50m go right over another stile down to a gate by a telegraph pole and the house beyond. Here, the right of way bears right along the driveway to the road where a right turn leads to Fownhope past the church, with the remains of its combined stocks and whipping post in the churchyard wall.

15

Ballingham village circular

Distance 4km **Time** 1 hour 30
Terrain riverside path, woodland and
lanes, with a steep descent to the river
Map OS Explorer 189 **Access** no bus service

**Step back in time and enjoy this now
tranquil countryside, which once
thronged with busy rural life.**

Ballingham is now a quiet village
tucked away to the west of one of the
sweeping loops of the River Wye between
Hereford and Ross. As with many villages
in this part of Herefordshire its
population has diminished over the last
hundred years, though there are hints of
its former significance, such as
Ballingham Hall whose stone frontage
and gables can be seen from the end of
the lane by the church. The blank panels
with their ovals are a sign of its origin
from the years after the Restoration in
1660, and the adjacent modern farm
buildings highlight the agricultural
changes that have taken place in more
recent years.

The walk itself starts from the
sandstone church of St Dubricius, a Celtic
saint of the 6th century, and goes up the
lane past the village hall, formerly the
school, towards the centre of the village,
with its green and pond. The lane
opposite leads to Ballingham Chapel, a
20th-century construction, and beyond to
the ancient settlement of Ballingham Hill.
The left fork is known as Saycells Path
and it leads to the farm of the same name.
The Saycells are a family whose earliest
recorded connection with the village
stretches back to the 13th century and the
whole place still has the feel of working
countryside, though the throngs of
agricultural workers have long gone.

Near the top of the lane, before the farm
at a path T-junction, turn right down past

◂ St Dubricius' churchyard at Ballingham

a house and then descend steeply along the edge of woodland and across the lane known as the King's Way, a medieval route which still runs parallel to the River Wye. Here, turn downstream along the riverbank, passing Mancell's Ferry house opposite. There are often wigwams in the field here and it's a good place to have a picnic on the riverbank. The path soon enters Ballingham Wood where it meets the river.

At the far end of the wood, keep to the right-hand side of the field, still following the edge of Ballingham Wood, with good views ahead to Capler Hill and its hill fort. At the wood's eastern end, bear right through a gate and climb steps steadily back uphill along the southern edge of the wood in a westerly direction, from where the spire of Ballingham church can be seen across the fields. The brambles lining the edge of the wood here are good for blackberrying in late summer or early autumn. The path passes through a gate and along the edge of a field to reach the road. Here a left turn uphill brings you to the buildings of Dunn's Farm and Mayview Farm, from where a path through the hedge on the left leads over the field in the direction of the church – there are often cows here with calves; if so, it might be an idea to follow the lane to the village centre and retrace steps past the village hall to the church.

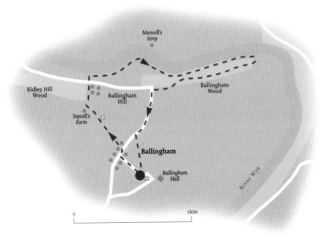

King's Caple and Foy meanders

Distance 15km **Time** 4-5 hours
Terrain field paths and lanes
Map OS Explorer 189 **Access** bus (37) from
Hereford and Ross; King's Caple is a
request detour stop

**This walk weaves its way among some of
the largest meanders of the River Wye,
crossing the river on picturesque
footbridges and passing through several
pretty hamlets. A detour to How Caple
Court and Gardens is possible.**

The church in King's Caple occupies the
former bailey of a Norman castle whose
motte, known as Caple Tump, stands
opposite. Some years ago in the
churchyard near the cross a grim discovery
was made of a plague pit, probably dating
to the Black Death of 1348. The walk heads
towards the centre of the village along
what was once a Roman Road known as
Caple Street, passing the impressive
red-brick King's Caple Court. The

name of the house and village recall that
local allegiance was once directly to the
kings of England, rather than to the
ecclesiastical authority of nearby
Hereford Cathedral.

At the crossroads turn right (SP Sellack
Boat) down the lane and at the sharp left
bend continue ahead to the River Wye
and across the suspension bridge, which
was paid for by public subscription in
1895 and replaced the old ferry and ford –
a story is still told about the vicar who,
in order to carry out his ministry with
dry feet, used to criss-cross the river on
stilts. Across the fields is Sellack, with its
prominent church and a rare dedication
to St Tyssilio. From here, the route turns
left uphill along quiet lanes through
Baysham to Strangford Farm. Beyond, a
tractor track leads over fields along the
top of the broad ridge for just over 1km,
with panoramic views over the
river valley and the surrounding

hills. Where the track bends left downhill, continue ahead for 150m, then right through a gate and down to the lane at Foy, before turning right for the church.

St Mary's is built in a commanding position overlooking the river and its setting is made grander by the proximity of the 18th-century vicarage, Foye Hall. Inside the church are memorials to the Abrahall family, along with some curious images of hedgehogs. The walk now crosses the field at the rear of the church to the river, a pleasant place to pause for a rest or picnic, and follows it upstream to cross Foy Bridge, another elegant suspension bridge, this one built in 1921 after the previous bridge was washed away by a flood. A left turn along the route of the Wye Valley Walk soon reaches the small hamlet of Hole-in-the-Wall, whose unusual name probably recalls the siting of a post-house here in the 19th century, though some talk of a tunnel below the Wye linking religious houses as the origin of the name. A little beyond,

just before a cattle grid, the way bears left down to the riverside again, with a balconied fishing lodge on the opposite bank, and on to How Caple.

Here, it is possible to make a detour uphill, for just over 1km, to visit the renowned How Caple Court and Gardens. The onward route leaves the Wye Valley Walk just beyond the bridge and turns left through a field-gate uphill, passing to the right of the house ahead and continuing in a WSW direction up over fields and down to Seabournes Farm at Fawley. A detour downhill leads to the private Fawley Chapel and Fawley Court, once the home of John Kyrle, the famous benefactor of Ross. Across the lane and past the cowsheds, a bridleway leads into the fields beyond. After 1km, in the third field, the path descends left and then bears round to the right over the outflow of a small lake, before passing through a tunnel under the disused Ross to Hereford railway and up one more field to a cottage. Here, a left turn onto the lane soon leads back to the houses of King's Caple.

◀ Suspension bridge at Foy

Ross-on-Wye and Chase Wood

Distance 10km **Time** 3-4 hours
Terrain riverside paths, fields and
steep slopes in Chase Wood
Map OS Explorer 189 **Access** bus (34) from
Monmouth and (37) from Hereford

**Retrace the river courses, ancient and
modern, around Ross before an
exhilarating ascent to the top of
Chase Wood.**

As 'Gate of the Wye', Ross has long been
associated with the river that winds its
way across the low ground to the west.
Indeed, an ancient river meander south of
Chase Wood suggests that millions of
years ago the sandstone outcrop on which
the town stands would have been almost
surrounded by the river. Nowadays there
are still extensive floods, though the town
has also long been known for its reliable
climate and houses one of the oldest
manual weather stations in the country.
The centre of Ross is dominated by the
red sandstone of the Market Hall, from
where the walk starts.

At the far end of the High Street, use
Wye Street to descend to the river. The
riverside path leads downstream to
Wilton, with its bridge and castle across
the water. The castle was a casualty of the
Royalists in the Civil War; its siting on low
ground is curious, but it predates the late
16th-century bridge by at least 300 years, so
it most likely guarded an ancient ford here.
The path continues over the bridge, with
an old river cliff away to the left, and after
1km veers away from the river to the corner
of the wood ahead. You soon cross the
driveway of Cubberley House, beyond
which a field-edge path leads to The
Homme farm.

Turn left down the farm's driveway and
right at the road, soon passing a cross in
woodland on the right and new Hom
Church on the left – the 'Cross in the
Woodland' is of unknown origin but may
mark the site of an old chapel. Just past the
entrance to Hill Court, the route turns left
up the driveway to the picturesque black
and white timbers of Old Hill Court and a
lane beyond. A dog-leg right then left takes

you over the fields of Coughton Marsh, with views to Chase Wood ahead on the left and Howle Hill on the right. The gap marks the line of the ancient meander of the River Wye. Now supporting fruit-growing, the whole of this low-lying area used to be the river's watercourse. On passing under electricity lines bear slightly right and the path soon reaches the B4234. Here, a detour right for 500m leads to the entrance to Coughton Marsh SSSI, a small area of marsh woodland of historical and biological interest because it is the only area of plateau alder woodland left in the lower Wye Valley.

The walk bears left into Coughton, right at the bend (SP Howle Hill) and through the village, which now occupies the ancient riverbed, passing a former Cider House which used also to be the tollhouse when this turnpike road was first built. Just before the last buildings, turn left onto the route of the Wye Valley Walk. Head up across fields into Chase Wood, where the path ascends very steeply to the hill fort at the top, and round its east side on which the earthworks are well-defined. Towards the north end, the track descends, with views to the Malvern Hills, past Hill Farm into Merivale Wood, a wildlife reserve managed by Herefordshire Nature Trust. Just beyond the entrance-gate turn left, off the Wye Valley Walk, onto a path which winds its way down through the wood, steeply at times, to a track at the bottom. Turn right to a metal kissing-gate and then left along the field edge, with views left to Garway Hill. Cross over the line of the disused railway and continue into the housing estate, bearing right along Merivale Lane past Merivale House. At the T-junction turn left and then right at the top of this road to return to the centre of Ross.

◂ Looking across river meadows to Ross-on-Wye

To the southwest of Hereford, and reaching southwards to Monmouth, is an ancient area of rolling hills and river valleys. Bounded on the north by the Worm Brook and in the east by the Wye river valley, it encloses an area extending southwards to the Monnow and Trothy Valleys. Hidden amongst its maze of narrow, winding lanes are the scenic villages of Kilpeck and Skenfrith, the hills of Orcop and Garway, and the distinctive rural landscape of scattered woods and field hedgerows. In former times, much of this area was known as Archenfield, or Ergyng, a name which itself may be derived from the Roman settlement of Ariconium at Weston under Penyard near Ross. It was a Welsh enclave, largely within what is now Herefordshire, where Welsh was spoken up to the start of the 20th century, testament to which is the number of places still with Welsh names.

Old road sign at Dingestow ▶

Archenfield and the Monnow and Trothy Valleys

STATION ¼
MITCHEL TROY 2½
RAGLAN 4

LLANDEILO ·
CROESENY 5½

23

Inn and out of Kilpeck

Distance 3km **Time** 1 hour **Terrain** lanes
and fields **Map** OS Explorer 189 **Access** bus
(Stagecoach X4) from Hereford and
Abergavenny stops at Wormford on
the A465, 2km west of Kilpeck

**Stroll around one of Herefordshire's
most historic villages before circling the
ancient fields and woods to the south.
This route is short enough to be ideal
before, or after, a visit to the pub.**

Kilpeck is one of the most celebrated
and popular villages in Herefordshire. Its
church draws visitors from far afield and
there is plenty to look at. The semi-
circular apse at the east end hints at its
Norman origins, but the carvings on the
doorway of its south porch and the corbel

table beneath the eaves are what most
come to see. There are 85 grotesque
medieval motifs to spot and some gaps
where a number of others have been
removed over the centuries, perhaps from
a more modern sense of propriety.

To the east of the church stands the
remains of a Norman motte and bailey
castle whose walls and moat invite
exploration. To the north is a helpful
information board and viewing spot, from
where the outline of the ancient village
stockade can be traced.

The village is a delight to wander
through and, though the school has long
since closed, the pub is experiencing a
new lease of life as the Kilpeck Inn, with a
warm welcome for walkers. Just by the old

◀ The south door of St Mary's and
St David's Church at Kilpeck

school, beyond the pub, a lane leads
off left and takes you up the hill.
Many of the lanes in this area
connect with the old trackway that
runs along the ridge ahead. Its
antiquity can only be guessed at, but
it may well stretch back to the Bronze
Age or even to Neolithic times. You
soon pass the village hall, where
there is ample parking and a contact
telephone number is posted for
non-hall users to check whether
parking is available that day.

The lane meanders uphill
and in 350m there is a track
off right which leads to
Dippersmoor Farm. Just
before the buildings take the
path left, off the track and into
the adjacent field, and pass
above an old timber and brick long
barn. The farm was originally
Dippersmoor Manor and of interest
architecturally as it is 15th-century
cruck construction, where both the walls
and the roof are supported on huge
curved beams.

Continue across the field to the rear of
the buildings, through a gap into a second
one and curve round to the right above a
delightful tree-lined dell. This area has
been signed as a game and wildlife
conservation area and it is requested that
dogs are kept on a lead here. The path
now reaches Dippersmoor Wood and
bears right along its southern edge, with

views ahead to the ridges of the Black
Mountains – and with the sun setting
behind these hills it is perhaps easy to see
how they got their name. At the bottom
of this field, bear left along the hedge for
50m and then turn right through a gate
into the field below.

In the bottom right-hand corner of this
field, the path leads northeastwards for
500m, alongside a hedge over a further
three fields, to reach the road just to the
south of Kilpeck. Here, turn right and
soon reach the old school and the centre
of the village.

The Garren Valley and Orcop Hill

Distance 4km **Time** 1 hour
Terrain undulating lanes and fields
Map OS Explorer 189 **Access** bus from
Hereford (412 direct, or 416 stops at Orcop
Turn on the A466, 1.5km to NE)

**Wander among the hidden folds
and meadows of the Garren Valley.
This one is great for kids and grown-ups
– the only decision is before or after a
visit to the pub.**

Orcop Hill is one of the highest points
on a chain of hills between the valleys of
the River Monnow, to the south, and the
Worm Brook, to the north. It is sited in
often bypassed countryside, equidistant
from Hereford, Ross and Monmouth
18km away. This scattered settlement,
which stretches south to Orcop village,
used to boast five pubs. Now, only
The Fountain remains, where parking is
available with permission. This pub
traces its name to the nearby Copywell
(or Coppice Well). Until the 1960s it was
the main source of water in the area,
requiring the inhabitants of the
Garren Valley to ferry their water for
considerable distances.

The walk starts from the Baptist Chapel
with its small graveyard opposite the inn
and heads uphill, taking the first road on
the left. Shortly, at a T-junction, bear left
for 500m round the left bend, and just
beyond the driveway to Quarry Farm take
a path left over a stile into a field. Follow
the top edge of this field to a stile hidden
in the far top corner. Cross into the next
field, and bear left downhill and through

the hedgeline into the field below. Here, the views open out to Orcop village and round to Garway Hill as you descend southwest over more fields. Local folklore tells the story of how the inhabitants of this valley had a lucky escape from the Devil. In one of their feuding contests, the giant Jack O'Kent and the Devil were vying to dam the valley in order to make an enormous fishpond and they began ferrying huge boulders as they jumped from hilltop to hilltop. However, they dropped their stones while landing on the summit of Garway Hill. The stones rolled down the south side and the place where they came to rest has since been known as White Rocks.

As the slope levels off, go through a gateway to the far side of the field to reach a crosspaths. Here is the site of the former Stradway Farm – the buildings are still marked on the map, though the farmer dismantled the farmhouse some years ago and surprisingly little evidence remains of what was a substantial building and cider mill. On clear, sunny days it is a tranquil spot, ideal now for a picnic or rest. To continue, turn left across the stile towards the woodland ahead on the left, where the field narrows. The edge of the woodland leads to a stile at the bottom of the field into a copse. Cross over a stream and through the copse to a

field. Here, turn left and follow the field edge with the stream on the left in trees.

The path soon crosses back over the stream, becoming a track which leads to and through Great Ynys Farm. *Ynys* is the Welsh word for 'island' and one theory for the origin of the name is that at one time the stream from the Copywell divided and flowed around both sides of the buildings, thus isolating the farm in mid-stream. The track now continues up to the road, where a left turn uphill soon reaches Orcop Hill.

◀ Looking south across the Garren Valley

Garway Hill and Jack O'Kent

Distance 9km Time **3-4 hours**
Terrain **lanes and fields; the high ground of Garway Hill can be confusing in mist**
Map **OS Explorer 189** Access **bus (X4) from Hereford or Abergavenny to Monmouth Cap stop, 3km west of starting point**

Walk in the footsteps of the giant Jack O'Kent and see seven counties from the best viewpoint the Monnow Valley has to offer.

Jack O'Kent is a figure intimately associated with Kentchurch. Some say that he was a giant wizard in league with the devil who had sold his soul in exchange for supernatural powers and that he built the bridge over the Monnow below Grosmont in just a single night, into the bargain short-changing the devil out of the due payment of the first living soul to set foot on it by throwing a bone

across, which was duly chased by a dog. Others record the tale that he is buried in the very walls of the church, so that being 'neither in nor out' his soul might be confined and not snatched by the devil. In nearby Kentchurch Park, there is even his own oak tree, reputedly a thousand years old and the largest in the Wye Valley, with a girth of over 11m.

From the church 1km east of Grosmont Bridge, head north along the road and take the first right along a lane to Bannut Tree Farm, with Kentchurch Park on the right. Just beyond the farm, take the path off right, which rises to a line of mature oaks and alongside a former sunken trackway into a copse to pass below Court-a-Grove Farm. Now the route crosses a series of six fields uphill in an easterly and then ENE direction (in the second field bear slightly left into the dip and through a copse above some springs to cross a

◄ Wild horses on Garway Hill

footbridge and stile into the next field).

On reaching the road, turn right and soon pass above a baptist chapel with views north to Aconbury Hill. When the road bends back left and Garway Hill communications mast is seen ahead, turn right up a track. At the top of the rise, bear left up through woodland past the communications mast onto the open slopes of Garway Hill to its triangulation point and old pill box. You can reputedly see seven counties on a clear day, but don't take your eye off your sandwiches, as the white mountain horses and the sheep are wise to what visitors bring them. The horses survive on the common all year round, getting their water from nearby Black Pool, which not only mysteriously lasts all year with no visible spring but also provides a breeding ground for the rare and protected great-crested newt. The hill is a haven for wildlife and has never been ploughed. There are said to be over 70 species of bird, including skylark, song

thrush and yellowhammer and it's a great habitat for butterflies.

Descend the far south side of the hill with views ahead to Dawn of the Day. On reaching the track near White Rocks – you might hear the 'hoo-hoo-hoo' or harsh 'kewick' of a thriving group of tawny owls here – turn right down past Little Castlefield, whose name recalls the former site of a Roman camp and road 1km to the southwest, near Castlefield Farm just above the Monnow. Now descend for just over 1km across fields, at first in a westerly direction, passing above a karting track and Little Corras Farm with views ahead to the Black Mountains. Then bear more to the right and aim for the left edge of the woodland ahead, before dropping down to the left to reach the road. Here, turn right and follow the lane, known now to some as the 'English Road', for a little over 1km back to Kentchurch, passing an ancient ford over the River Monnow which is still used by farm vehicles.

Skenfrith and Llanrothal

Distance **9km** Time **3 hours**
Terrain **riverside and woodland paths
with a climb out of the Monnow Valley**
Map **OS Explorer OL 14**
Access **no bus service**

**Explore the historic village of Skenfrith
before venturing down the secluded
valley of the River Monnow.**

Clustered round a bend of the River
Monnow, the village of Skenfrith, with its
castle and church, provides one of the most
picturesque settings of Welsh rural life in
existence today. There is even a community
shop, staffed by volunteers at weekends
ever-ready to supply tea and ice cream.
Parking is available on what was once the
stone-revetted moat of the medieval castle,
one of the so-called trilateral castles (the
others are Grosmont and White Castle),
and there are a number of information
boards to help with exploration.

Just beyond the pub, The Bell, the road
to Ross crosses the River Monnow over the
stone bridge, built in 1824 at a time when
travel by coach and horse was still the
only practical means of long-distance
transport and a reminder of the pub's role
as a coaching inn – the inaugural run of
the world's first railway passenger service
was still six years away. A path leads off
right in a northeasterly direction over
fields beside the river for 1.5km to the
grounds of Sand House. Now it is a
tranquil walk, thick with balsam in late
summer, but the rediscovery of the
medieval quay at Skenfrith Castle has
pointed to the importance of the river as a
means of transporting goods from
Monmouth and beyond. It is likely that
flat-bottomed barges would have been
used, hauled upriver by horses or gangs of
men in harness.

Passing in front of the house, bear left
over a footbridge and left again into
woodland to follow a waymarked path

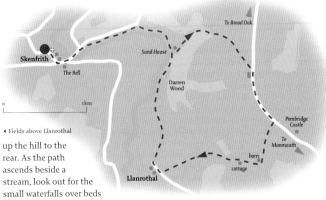

◀ Fields above Llanrothal

up the hill to the rear. As the path ascends beside a stream, look out for the small waterfalls over beds of tufa, formed when limestone dissolved in water is deposited on rocks and debris in the stream. Cross over a forestry track to continue uphill, through a gate and over a footbridge to a stile. Bear right and shortly leave the woodland to go over three fields in a southeasterly direction to the top of the hill with views back to Garway Hill and Dawn of the Day (go diagonally left up the first field or follow the right-hand edges if ploughed; in the third one aim for the bungalow).

At the road, turn right over the brow of the hill and down into the dip, with views northeast to the Malvern Hills and the Monnow Valley to the right. Ahead can be seen Pembridge Castle – a restored 13th-century fortified manor house and in 1679 the scene of the arrest of the Catholic martyr John Kemble. By then an elderly priest, Kemble was implicated in Titus Oates' allegations of a papist plot to kill the king, Charles II. Arrested by John Scudamore of nearby Kentchurch, he was tried in London and then returned to Hereford to be hanged. One of Kemble's hands is still preserved at Hereford; his body rests nearby in the churchyard of St Mary's, Welsh Newton, and local Roman Catholics make an annual pilgrimage to his grave.

From the dip, bear right through a field opening and take the lower of a pair of paths bearing right down to a stream in a wooded dell and into the field beyond. Pass under the electricity lines and in 50m go right through a field gate and continue to the barn ahead. A right turn beside the banked hedge leads down to a house and a track to Llanrothal.

At the lane, turn right and go past Llanrothal Court to a field gate. Now cross four fields, with the River Monnow nearby on the left, and continue into the woodland ahead, where a path soon brings you to Sand House once again. From here, the outward route is followed back to Skenfrith.

31

The Trothy and the lost abbey

Distance **4km** Time **1 hour 30**
Terrain **lanes and fields, which can
get muddy** Map **OS Explorer OL14**
Access **no bus service**

**This short circuit takes in some of the
most secluded and tranquil countryside
the Trothy Valley has to offer, with
pleasant walking by the river and great
views from the ridge above.**

Llanvihangel-Ystern-Llewern is one of
the most out-of-the-way spots in the
Trothy Valley and is found 8km west of
Monmouth near Onen on the B4233
Abergavenny road. The name of the place
most likely means 'St Michael's by the
Marshy Bend of the River' and hints at its
low-lying location near the River Trothy.
There is room for a few cars to park just

by the church. Offa's Dyke Path runs
through here and the church is kept
locked when not in use.

From the church, walk up the road to
the bend and bear left on a track on the
route of Offa's Dyke Path (ODP), with
the River Trothy below on the left. After
300m, just before farm buildings, bear
left across a footbridge into riverside
meadows, which are liable to flooding
and can be muddy in places in wet
conditions. However, in dry conditions
in spring and summer it makes for a
picture-postcard stroll beside the twisting
Trothy. After 750m, as the second field
broadens out, look for a marker post by
the river indicating a right turn up the
steep bank to cut the corner of the
third field.

◄ Above Llanvihangel-Ystern-Llewern looking west

Now, away from the river, continue on ODP over three more fields in a southeasterly direction to the road above Abbey Bridge. The name of the bridge recalls the siting, a little to the southeast, of former Grace Dieu Abbey. It was another Cistercian foundation but now, unlike nearby Tintern Abbey and Abbey Dore, not a stone of this retreat remains visible and its actual location is uncertain. Quite why Grace Dieu vanished is lost to history, but there still lingers the sense of isolation that the Cistercians must have been seeking in establishing a monastery in this valley.

Now turn right, off the route of ODP, uphill past Abbey Cottage and then right again, just over the brow of the hill, along a lane which rises and falls, giving good views of the surrounding countryside. After a little over 1km, at a junction, the lane bends uphill to the right (north) and passes through a delightful copse of woodland before descending, with views to the hills of the Skirrid and the Graig, round some steep bends to the start.

Monmouth and the King's Wood

Distance 6km **Time** 2 hours
Terrain lanes, fields and woodland
slopes **Map** OS Explorer OL14 **Access**
buses (69) from Chepstow, (416) from
Hereford and (34) from Ross

**Stride out and enjoy the high ground
above Monmouth before exploring one of
the most historic market towns in Britain.**

Just before the River Monnow enters the
Wye at Monmouth, it arcs a great bow. On
the higher ground enclosed by this
meander are the remains of the Norman
castle, and a millennium before that the
Romans had sited their military camp of
Blestium here. Recent excavations, in
particular behind the shops on Monnow
Street, have yielded a plethora of artefacts
and theories about the town's past. The
Nelson Museum at the top end of town is
well worth a visit for those wanting to
explore the local history further.

The walk starts from the lower end of
Monnow Street at the Monnow Bridge
over the River Monnow. Its 13th-century
fortified gatehouse, the only surviving
one in Britain, is one of the iconic features
of the lower Wye Valley and gives a good
viewpoint back over the town. Vehicles
were able to pass through the central arch
until just a few years ago, but access has
been improved, if not the view, by the
addition of a steel and concrete bridge a
little downstream. It is one of four gates
into the town and before the current
stone structure there was a wooden
bridge here – its remains were dated by
tree-ring analysis to the 1170s. The south
side of the bridge marks the boundary
with Overmonnow, known as Cappers
Town as it was the centre for the making
of the famous Monmouth caps. Headgear
does not carry the same significance
today, but more familiar are the
muntlings – a type of street-skirmishing
in which gangs of youths from Cappers
Town met the Up-Town boys for fisticuffs
on the bridge at the end of May. There was
a return fixture sometime in June. The
practice was officially banned in 1828.

Away from the town on the left is the old red sandstone church of St Thomas. Turn right along Drybridge Street and pass in front of Drybridge House along Rockfield Road. Just past the fire station, look out on the left for Watery Lane and follow the route of Offa's Dyke Path which soon bears to the left away from the new housing estate. The lane narrows and, soon after it bends right, go left through the open entrance to a large field, and then pass under electricity lines across the field to the buildings of Bailey Pitt Farm (if crops block the way, use the field edge next to the lane a little further on). At the former farm, cross onto the lane and turn left to pass between the hedge, with its small stream, and the buildings.

At the top of the garden, the path enters the King's Wood and becomes a bridleway, which climbs up through the mixed woodland. On reaching a second forestry track, turn left round the bend and take the next track on the left, which soon levels out and contours the hill's eastern slopes through Hunt Grove, with

widening views of the Wye Valley below. The very top of the hill and its triangulation pillar can be reached via a short detour up to the right.

After the track bends right on the south side of the hill, turn sharp left downhill onto a bridleway to reach the edge of the woodland at a pair of gates. Here, a double line of mature oak trees leads to the bottom of the field and, hidden on the left, a stile into Lady Grove Wood. A pleasant woodland track descends to the edge of the wood. Here, cross into a field and along the fence to a double stile down into the next field. From here, you can use the spire of St Mary's Church in Monmouth as a guide over a series of fields downhill, tracking a little to the left as the ground levels out, and in just over 1km you reach the outskirts of Monmouth. Pass under electricity lines and then between buildings and finally houses. The path keeps to the right of the former grounds of Drybridge House and emerges onto Wonastow Road. Here, turn left and then right to return to Monnow Street.

◀ The Monnow Bridge at Monmouth

Dingestow and the Trothy

Distance **4km** Time **1 hour 30**
Terrain **fields and woodland**
Map **OS Explorer OL14** Access **bus (83)
from Monmouth and Abergavenny or
(60) from Newport**

**Wander along the water meadows
and up the slopes of the Trothy Valley
– a great family walk with lots to see
and explore.**

The delightful village of Dingestow is
set amongst the meadows of the River
Trothy, just above the point where the
river turns eastwards on its approach to
Monmouth and the Wye. To the northeast
there is high ground, which gives a
commanding viewpoint deeper into Wales.

From the centre of the village, pass

Bridge Farm and Salter's Cottage and
turn right along the lane past the
parish church, which is dedicated to
St Dingat. This is one of only three
dedications to the Celtic saint and
tradition has it that he is buried here.
The list of vicars goes back to 1390 and
the remains of Dingestow Castle a little
further down the lane have been dated to
1182, when the timber buildings were
burnt down. The tump of the castle is
accessible to the public through a
gateway on the left.

Just beyond the tump, take the footpath
on the right into the fields to the west of
the Trothy. Head north for 1km over five
fields, with the river never far away on the
right (halfway through the third field,

◄ In the fields above Dingestow

bear a little left away from the river to find the stile). The area is prone to flooding, but in good weather during spring and summer there is very pleasant walking here. At the top of the fifth field, with the buildings of Lower Llantrothy away on the left, cross the Trothy on a footbridge beneath a large oak tree.

Now turn sharp right for a short way along the river and, where it bends south, head up the slope ahead to a gate into the field beyond. Cross diagonally to the top of this field and go through a gate onto a track which leads through Treowen Wood, where it is often possible to surprise fallow deer. In 300m, at a track junction, turn right and approach the rear of Treowen House, with good views to the south and west. The house today is one of the most impressive private houses in Monmouthshire. When it was built in the early 1600s, of pink Old Red Sandstone, its height and design must have been imposing, set as it is on the high ground overlooking the Trothy Valley.

Pass the main house and, just beyond the last buildings, turn right off the driveway to the house through a gate and across two fields to descend to Mill Wood. Head down on a clear path through the wood. Just above the road, on the right, is a mound, the remains of a motte and bailey, and well worth exploring, as are the small dells on the other side of the path. At the road, turn right over a bridge across the Trothy to return to Dingestow.

37

OF YOUR CHARITY PRAY for the SOULS of the FAMILY of PROBERT of TRELECH and PENALLT

The lost treasures of Troy

Distance **8km** Time **2 hours 30**
Terrain **fields, woodland paths and lanes**
Map **OS Explorer OL14** Access **buses (69)
from Chepstow, (416) from Hereford and
(34) from Ross-on-Wye**

**Climb the high ground to the south of
Monmouth for extensive views before
reaching the hidden settlement of
Penallt perched on the hillside above the
Wye Valley.**

From the old Monnow Bridge with its
gatehouse, follow the line of the River
Monnow along Cinderhill Street, past the
new bridge, under the dual carriageway
and up to the Mitchell Troy road (B4293).
Turn left along the pavement, and at the
bend bear left down the track to Troy
Farm. Just beyond a bridge over the River
Trothy, which flows into the Wye a little
further on, pass Troy House.

The north front's unusual number of
storeys (three rather than two), 13 bays

and double flight of steps give it an
imposing look. It was built in the 1680s at
a cost of £3000 by the first Duke of
Beaufort as a second home for his son
once he married, their main residence in
Monmouth being Great Castle House,
built only the previous decade. For much
of the 20th century, the nuns of the Order
of the Good Shepherd ran the place as a
school for errant girls and there are now
plans to turn it into apartments.

The current state of the house is less
grand, though the Trothy still meanders
through its grounds.

At the rear of the farm, a sunken track
leads uphill into fields. In the second field
bear diagonally left up to a stile into
woodland, with a great view scanning
west to east over the Trothy Valley and in
the distance the Black Mountains, the
King's Wood, and the hills above Garway,
with the valley of the Monnow in the
centre, then the Buckholt stretching

To Ross

River Wye

Monnow Bridge

Monmouth

0   1km

To Newport

River Trothy

Troy House

Livox Woods

To Chepstow

Penallt

Birches Road

◄ Stained glass window in
the Old Church at Penallt

northwards, the high ground of Welsh
Newton Common, and, curling round the
foot of the Kymin, the River Wye. The
route bears left and then right – look out
for the marker post – up through Troy
Park Wood over the shoulder of the hill
and beyond into some small fields.

At a gate just before a stone barn, bear
left down to Penallt Church. This is the
village's old church, unusual in having no
known dedication, and is set in a lofty
position above the Wye Valley, though the
size of the graveyard hints that it was not
always so isolated a place. Inside, on the
west wall, hangs the royal coat of arms of
Queen Anne with the motto 'semper
eadem' (always the same); originally it
was hung facing the congregation, an
imposing reminder of the political power
of the monarch, then recently
demonstrated in the 1707 Act of Union of
England and Scotland; or perhaps more
accurately it was an Act which linked
Scotland with the 1536 Union of England

and Wales. There is also a strange
diagonal passageway and arch from the
aisle to the chancel.

Beyond the lych gate, look out for an old
chestnut tree (the village stocks were
located here) and, opposite, a stone
mounting block. The route turns left here
down Birches Road for just under 500m
and then bears left, past the entrance to
Hillside Farm, onto a sunken track (look
out for the marker post on the telegraph
pole). The track weaves its way down
through Washing's Wood to the River Wye.

Now follow the bank upstream and
along the edge of Livox Wood, passing the
remains of a series of small weirs before
emerging onto the flood meadows.
Nearing the Trothy once more, climb the
small knoll ahead to a track, which leads
back to Troy Farm and the outward route.

To the south of Ross-on-Wye, at Goodrich, the River Wye does something extraordinary. Many rivers in Britain, as they near their end, become slow and sluggish, developing sweeping meanders banked by floodplains or spreading out into channels to form a delta. By contrast, in its final miles the Wye enters a gorge, at times surprisingly steep-sided and more reminiscent of one of the great continental rivers of Europe. Coldwell Rocks, Yat Rock, the Seven Sisters, Shorn Cliff and Wyndcliff, Ban-y-Gor and the Apostles Rocks, and the crags of Wintour's Leap all tower above the river before the Wye slips into the Severn at the Caldicot Levels. The result is the formation of some of the most dramatic riverside scenery in Britain. It was for this reason that from the late 18th century many artists, philosophers and writers visited this hidden river valley in search of the sublime and the picturesque. William Gilpin has become synonymous with the Wye Tour from Ross to Chepstow and famous for laying out the complex principles of foreground, background and colour which have so influenced appreciation of what makes beautiful riverscape. Yet the towns and villages of Monmouth, Redbrook, Brockweir, Tintern and Chepstow, and all the settlements along the river's banks, are more than picture-postcard places, each with their historical record stretching back over hundreds, if not thousands, of years. The result is one of the richest and most rewarding areas for walking and exploration on foot.

Cliffs of the River Wye at Chepstow ▶

The Wye Gorge

Coppet Hill and Coldwell Rocks

Distance 12km **Time** 3 hours 30
Terrain lanes and riverside paths, with
steep slopes on Coppet Hill
Map OS Explorer OL14 **Access** bus (34)
from Ross-on-Wye and Monmouth

**Hill and riverside combine to make this
the perfect half-day walk – or take a
picnic and make a lazy day of it.**

Perched on high ground between
sweeping loops of the River Wye,
Goodrich marks a significant change in
the landscape of the Wye Valley. From the
relatively flat and lazy lowlands upstream,
the river now twists and turns before
entering a gorge-like riverscape past
Coldwell Rocks on its way to Symonds Yat
and the cliffs of the Seven Sisters. For
good reason the Romans named it *Vaga*,
'the Wanderer'.

One of the main attractions of Goodrich
is the castle, just to the north of the
village centre where parking is available.
There is also a good village shop where
you can stock up on supplies for the walk.

From here, take the minor road to
Courtfield and Welsh Bicknor uphill over
the B4229 towards Coppet Hill. After 500m
you reach a fork in the road. Here, look
out for the path between the forks, up
steps through woodland and past
outcrops of pudding stone rocks – you
can clearly see pebbles embedded in the
rock. Climb fairly steeply to emerge from
the woods onto the well-defined north
ridge which leads to a triangulation point
and the base of a stone folly just beyond.
The views from here on a clear day are a
just reward for the effort of ascent.

Descend Coppet Hill's long south ridge
for 2.5km into woods beside a collapsed
drystone wall to reach fields beside the
River Wye, opposite the base of Coldwell
Rocks. This provides a good spot to rest
and watch the peregrine falcons which
breed high up on the cliffs. They have now
become a tourist attraction in their own
right and their presence is protected by
the RSPB, though this traditional
breeding site nearly saw the last of the

◀ The River Wye above
Coldwell Rocks

falcons in the 1960s
because of the effects of
pesticide poisoning.

The route now turns left
to follow the riverside path
upstream over fields and
through woods to reach
Welsh Bicknor in 3km,
along what must be one
of the most tranquil and
idyllic stretches of river
the Wye Valley has to
offer. A little before
Welsh Bicknor the
former Monmouth to
Ross railway crosses the
river from Lydbrook
Junction before disappearing into a
tunnel under the hill – look out for the
pill box on the left here. (*By crossing over the
river at this point, the English Bicknor walk,
page 44, can be joined.*) Just past the youth
hostel there is a fine Victorian restoration
of the church of St Margaret, which
houses a 14th-century tomb with an effigy
of Margaret Montacute. Outside there is a
plague cross, a reminder that even a
secluded spot like this did not escape the
harsh realities of rural life. It is curious to
note that Welsh Bicknor is in England and
sited to the east of English Bicknor which
lies across the river up the hill – the result
of the vagaries of the Wye and the border.

Follow the riverside path for 1km
further until you are opposite Lower
Lydbrook. At the apex of the river bend,

turn left along the line of an old route
uphill to Courtfield House. Here, the path
becomes a lane which follows the wall of
the house's grounds round to the left. You
can glimpse the rear of the 19th-century
house, which for centuries was the seat of
the Vaughan family. More recently it was a
retreat for the monks of the Mill Hill
Missionary Society. This society was itself
founded by Herbert Vaughan, who
became a cardinal of the Roman Catholic
Church and was responsible in 1895 for
the building of the new Westminster
Cathedral. Now the house stands empty.
The lane continues along the ridge with
broad views back down to the Wye and
beyond to the high ground of the Forest
of Dean. A little past Courtfield Farm, the
lane becomes a pleasant minor road and
in just over 2km leads back to Goodrich.

English Bicknor and Offa's Dyke

Distance **6km** Time **2 hours**
Terrain **fields, lanes and riverside paths**
Map **OS Explorer OL14** Access **bus (35)
from Ross and Monmouth**

**Step back through history in a place
where people have lived and worked the
land for the last 6000 years.**

English Bicknor is one of the oldest
settlements in the area. Today the most
visible remains of former times are the
Norman church and the moat of the 12th-
century motte and bailey castle which still
surrounds the church. A hint of even
greater antiquity is given by the oval
shape of the churchyard, pointing to the
presence of Saxon building, and the well-
preserved section of Offa's Dyke which
runs just below the village. In addition
local archaeologists have identified a
Roman settlement near the southern
edge of the village and flint tools have
been found, suggesting Neolithic peoples
inhabited the site. It is a great village to
explore before or after the walk which
begins from the car park near the school,
where there is also an excellent
information board.

A footpath passes to the left (west) of
the school and church, heading north
across fields, over the top of the hill to a
fence, and right along the field edge to
another stile just beyond the roadside
house. The route descends NNE between
strips of woodland along a broad ridge
over three fields. Here the path turns left
to reach the top of a lane down to the
road and the outskirts of Lower Lydbrook.

◀ Tombstone in churchyard of St Mary the Virgin at English Bicknor

Turn left onto the road and in 150m round the bend take the footpath left past a disused factory to the River Wye and under the disused railway bridge of the former Ross to Monmouth line. (*At this point the Coppet Hill walk may be joined by crossing the bridge and turning right.*) This is the site of Lydbrook Junction, where the Severn and Wye Railway joined to give access to the coalmines of the Forest of Dean.

Now follow the Wye Valley Walk riverside path downstream for just over 1km, between a picturesque Anglers' Hut on the left and a launching stage on the right and then over fields. This section by the river is one of the most pleasant riverside stretches and it is possible in various places to get down to the water's edge where there are some small strands, great for seeing the river close up or for cooling off the feet on a hot day. Just beyond a metal kissing gate, where the path enters woodland, leave the Wye Valley Walk and turn left along the disused railway track into a field. Here, the route bears to the right through a well-preserved section of Offa's Dyke, a reminder that the border is not far away and of the strategic importance to the dyke of the Wye.

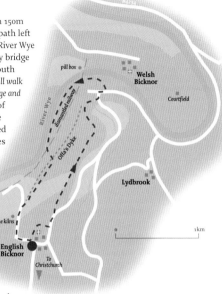

A bit of puff is now required to climb southwest over fields to a lane. Go left up the lane, in 200m passing a path which leads to the restored Rosemary Topping lime kilns. These have been recently restored, largely by a team of volunteers. The lane continues uphill to a junction, beyond which a detour can take you to Bicknor Court. To reach English Bicknor, turn left and a last pull uphill brings you back to the village.

King Arthur's Cave and the Seven Sisters

Distance shorter option 1.5km; longer
option 6km **Time** 1 hour or 2-3 hours
Terrain woodland and riverside paths,
lanes, cliff edges **Map** OS Explorer OL14
Access no bus service, but a cyclepath
from Monmouth leads to Biblins Bridge
and Symonds Yat (East), at which points
the walk can be joined

Explore the legendary King Arthur's Cave
before following the line of the Seven
Sisters, a series of limestone cliffs
hanging above the Wye Gorge. There is an
option to extend the walk to Symonds Yat
(East) with its famous Yat Rock
viewpoint and cross the river on a small
ferry. Take a torch for the caves.

From White Rocks Nature Reserve car
park by Doward Park Campsite, walk back
down the road past the entrance to the
campsite. A little further on take the first
track on the left downhill to an old
quarry. Here, bear to the right to continue
past a line of caves.

The last and largest is King Arthur's
cave with its double entrance and two
large chambers. Here, in 1695, a goatherd
discovered a large skeleton with the
remains of a spear; local legend claims it
was the body of King Arthur himself. In
1870 the Rev W S Symonds, one of the
founders of the local Woolhope
Naturalists' Field Club, unearthed the
bones of extinct mammals, including
mammoths and cave lions, which may
well have been gnawed by hyenas, along
with flint implements of Palaeolithic
people and Neolithic pottery, so adding to
the evidence establishing the antiquity of
humankind. He also found rolled river
pebbles, which could only have been
introduced by a river flowing 90m above
the present bed of the Wye. The animal
remains can be seen in Hereford Museum.

Rejoin the path which soon curves to
the left and descends gently until a small
band of limestone rocks appears on the
left. Bear left up through the rocks and

46

◄ Hand-pull ferry
  at Symonds Yat

along the top of
the Seven Sisters
cliff. Short side-
paths lead to the cliff
edges where there are sheer
drops from the top of the limestone
rock towers, on which rare species
associated with natural grassland
grow, and views along one of the
finest river gorges in southern Britain.

A little further on, in a dip, a path
leads off left uphill. The shorter
option follows this path, soon
passing to the right of the disused
White Rocks quarry before joining a
forest track up to Doward Park Campsite.

To take the longer option to Symonds
Yat, cross the dip and climb through a
second band of rocks until a wide forest
track is reached. Turn right downhill to
the Biblins campsite. Now cross the
suspension bridge and turn left on a
riverside track to reach the hotels and
houses of Symonds Yat just beyond a run
of rapids. From here, by a series steps, Yat
Rock can be reached, where peregrine
falcons, goshawks and buzzards can be
viewed. Recross the river by the small
hand-pull ferry, for which there is a small
charge. (If the river is in flood or to avoid
the ferry crossing, do not cross Biblins
bridge but follow a riverside path on the
Biblins side to reach the bank opposite
Symonds Yat.)

From the bank opposite Symonds Yat,
follow the twisting lane ahead uphill and,
just before a postbox, turn left up a
narrow path between houses to meet a
woodland track. Bear left, soon passing an
old quarry with a small memorial stone
on the right. Continue to climb, and take
the next path right uphill to soon pass a
cave on the right. Just beyond, as the path
levels out in front of a fenced-off area of
cave entrances, turn right. Follow this
track and its fence uphill as it curves to
the left, ignoring two other paths forking
right. The track soon levels off, with
open woodland on the left and an old
drystone wall boundary on the right.
At a crosspaths, continue straight ahead.
The track soon becomes a lane to take you
back to Doward Park Campsite.

47

Redbrook and the Newland meander

Distance 7km **Time** 2 hours **Terrain** tracks
and lanes **Map** OS Explorer OL14
Access bus (69) from Monmouth and
Chepstow

**A climb through woods from riverside
Redbrook leads to the picturesque village
of Newland, with its impressive church
known as the Cathedral of the Forest,
before retracing the route of an ancient
meander of the River Wye.**

The walk starts opposite the car park
and small recreation area at the Village
Stores. Take the rising lane to the left and
bear right in front of the school. Follow
the lane uphill and enter woodland where
the lane becomes a track. As the track
levels out, bear right onto an old
tramroad track.

The wood here is called Forge Wood – a
reminder that Redbrook was an important
industrial centre for smelting iron ore, for
which large amounts of charcoal were
needed. It is possible to see the remains
of charcoal and other workings in the
woods off the path. Continue ahead,
ignoring paths off right, to the top of the
slope to emerge from the woods.

Bear left and follow the track in a tree-
lined hollow way downhill to the
outskirts of Newland, to a sign off right
for a Restricted Byway (this is the start of
the return route). To enter Newland
village, continue ahead and take the first
lane on the left up Savage Hill to the
village centre and its All Saints Church.
The church, dating back to the 13th
century, is known locally as the Cathedral
of the Forest because of its size and
setting. Inside are a number of effigies
and monuments, including the Miners
Brass engraving. To the west of the church

is the former grammar school, now a private house; to the south is a row of almshouses established by the benefactor William Jones, a member of the Haberdashers' Livery Company.

To start the return, retrace steps to the Restricted Byway sign. Turn left along this lane, which soon turns into a track as the view opens out. On the left is the distinctive shape of a V-shaped river valley. Here the ancient Newland meander can be seen as it curves around to the right with remnants of old woodland on the slopes above. It is thought that the Wye once followed this course at a height 90m above its current level. Continue until you cross a small stone bridge over Valley Brook just before the buildings of Lodges Farm.

Follow the byway as it now turns right, off the track, over fields with Valley Brook below on the right. The byway curves right to Birt's Cottage and then starts the descent to recross Valley Brook at a drystone-walled bridge. Go past two large ponds to the point where the byway descends left. Leave the byway and take the right fork ahead along a wide footpath.

In the past the descent to Redbrook would have been very different, with clouds of smoke rising and the noise of industrial activity, most recently from the trains of the Wye Valley Railway which ran from Monmouth to Chepstow from 1876

to 1964, or from the Tinplate Works which only ceased production in 1962. These had succeeded the Copper Works at the start of the 18th century, when copper ore was shipped from Cornwall and up the Wye from Chepstow to the quayside in Redbrook – The Boat Inn across the old railway bridge serves as a reminder of the past reliance on river transportation. The woodlands on either side of Valley Brook would have been dotted with the small cottages and huts of charcoal burners whose livelihood depended on supplying fuel for the furnaces. Now the woodlands are managed and serene, providing a peaceful end to the walk. A little way down, the path again crosses Valley Brook and becomes a lane which leads back into Redbrook.

◀ Newland All Saints Church, the 'Cathedral of the Forest'

The mills of Whitebrook

Distance 4km **Time** 1 hour 30
Terrain some steep paths and tracks with
170m of ascent **Map** OS Explorer OL14
Access bus (65) from Chepstow and
Monmouth via Trellech joins the route at
the Narth

**Discover the Wye Valley's industrial past
among the ruins of two now secluded
and peaceful tributaries.**

The White Brook flows from the high
ground around Trellech and quickly
plunges through a steep-sided wooded
gorge which can only be glimpsed from
the River Wye below. Now the valley is a
tranquil spot full of delightful cottages
and bubbling streams. Yet there are many
hints of its less picturesque past. Virtually
every house is connected in some way to
the water-powered industries that became
established here from the start of the 17th
century, when a branch of Tintern
Wireworks was established. A century
later, papermaking was flourishing and
dotted around are dams, ponds and leats,
all connected to the mills and
warehouses. However, it was not to last
and by 1880 the boom was over.

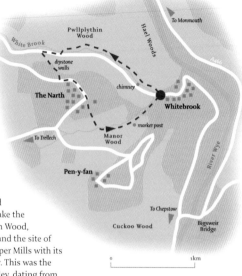

Today the valley is filled with greenery-covered ruins and restored private houses clustered around the narrow road which climbs steeply up the valley – there is some roadside parking at the top end of the village. Start the walk a little above the chapel in the middle of the village, and across the White Brook take the track left into Pwllplythin Wood, passing old mill houses and the site of the former Clearwater Paper Mills with its octagonal stone chimney. This was the first paper mill in the valley, dating from 1760, and was even fitted with a steam engine in the 1860s.

The track climbs gently through woods with the brook down on the left. Shortly after the track crosses the brook, it meets the road. Turn right and after 100m, just before the next house, turn sharp left uphill on a footpath. This old route, lined with drystone walls, climbs steeply through woodland to the Narth (ignore a footpath left after the path levels out). Now turn left along the road into the centre of the Narth.

Just round the right-hand bend, in the centre of the village, take a path on the left to Manorside. Descend gently, over a

crosspaths, to a metal kissing gate. Turn left and almost immediately right to continue the descent through woodland to a forest track and Manor Brook. Cross the brook and pick a way up the far bank to reach another forest track. Here, turn left and follow the brook downhill. After 200m, just beyond a prominent path branching right uphill, leave the track and take the signed path off left to continue downhill. Follow this path, which can be wet after rain, with Manor Brook down on the left until you reach a house. Here, the path becomes a track and soon arrives at a lane. Now turn left downhill to reach the centre of Whitebrook.

◀ Octagonal chimney of the former Clearwater Paper Mills at Whitebrook

Cleddon Falls and Catbrook

Distance **5km** Time **1 hour 30**
Terrain **woodland, fields, and lanes**
Map **OS Explorer OL14** Access **bus (69)
from Monmouth and Chepstow stops at
Llandogo, where there is a steep signed
route to the top of Cleddon Falls**

**Take life slowly and enjoy the woods,
views and waterfalls above Llandogo.**

This makes for an ideal family outing.
Just off the Tintern to Trellech road above
Llandogo, the car park at Whitestone
(GR525029) at the southern end of Bargain
Wood is a great place for a picnic and for
children of all ages to run around. There is
also a small play area with some wooden
climbing frames and posts.

Follow the Wye Valley Walk path
northwards on a broad track through
Bargain Wood, past three viewpoints, each
one giving a slightly different perspective

down to the Wye Valley. The woodland is
a delight at any time of year, but is
perhaps at its best in early spring or the
leaf-fall of autumn. Its name is something
of a misnomer and is thought to be a
corruption of 'bare gain', referring
derogatorily to the poor grazing to be had
here in former times, but there's plenty of
scope for exploring off the path here.

Where the track bends sharp left, bear
right, still on the Wye Valley Walk, and
soon descend between moss-covered
boundary walls to the houses of Cleddon
and its falls. The approach from Llandogo
requires a steep climb of over 150m
through the woods, but on this route you
arrive at the top of the falls, where the
stream leaves the gently sloping plateau.

The point at which this stream, and
many others in the valley, suddenly
plunge down marks what may have been

◄ Cleddon Falls above Llandogo

the level of an ancient sea, before the passing of successive ice ages caused sea levels to drop and the course of the Wye to become entrenched in the gorge we see today. It is possible to descend right, with care, down steps to gain a clearer view of the falls.

Just beyond, at the road, leave the Wye Valley Walk path and turn left with Cleddon Hall soon visible on the right, where the philosopher Bertrand Russell was born, and after 500m, at a crossroads, turn left to a junction, passing the lower end of Cleddon Bog. If time and footwear allow, the bog is worth exploring, though it is a sensitive site, being the largest surviving area of heath that used to cover much of the Trellech plateau.

To continue, cross the road, dog-legging left then right onto a track into Ninewells Wood – now much of it is conifer plantation but the wells around its perimeter are still there. Go uphill round the right bend and in 200m turn left onto a crosspath. In 100m fork left and soon reach the edge of the woodland.

The landscape now takes on a sudden change, with many of the field boundaries made of drystone walling, and even the stiles are of stone, giving the area a feel similar to that of the southern part of the Peak District. Cross a stone stile and follow the drystone wall on the left over two fields with views ahead to the Severn Estuary. In the third field, go diagonally right and cross the next to the corner of the copse ahead. Descend southwest through the wood and the small fields beyond to Catbrook. Here, a left turn downhill along the road for 1km makes for pleasant walking. Finally, bear right at the junction which is just a short distance above the turning to Whitestone car park.

Brockweir and The Hudnalls

Distance **6km** Time **2 hours**
Terrain **byways, woodland and riverside
paths; ascent of 200m** Map **OS Explorer
OL14** Access **bus (69) from Monmouth
and Chepstow stops on the A466**

**Follow the twisting lanes made by
woodland squatters as you ascend
St Briavels Common and walk in the
footsteps of former bargemen beside
the River Wye.**

The former riverside port of Brockweir
lies on the Gloucestershire side of the
River Wye and, until the current bridge
was built at the start of the 20th century,
the crossing had to be made by ferry. At
one time the village had over a dozen inns
and drinking houses to meet the demand
of all the shipbuilders and workers,
though now just one remains. The barge-

trade was the main business here in the
19th century and it would have been a
common sight to see teams of men in
harness pulling flat-bottomed barges
laden with coal or iron upstream to
Monmouth and even as far as Hereford.
It can be a popular place for summer
tourists and there is some parking near
the top end of the village; alternatively
park in the layby on the A466 and walk
over the bridge.

Just beyond the bridge over the River
Wye, turn left along Underhill Road. Pass a
turning off left and a footpath off right
and, 100m beyond, turn right just before
Orchard Cottage onto a Restricted Byway
which leads uphill in a northerly direction
through an area known as The Hudnalls.
In origin this was common woodland and
an outlier of the Forest of Dean. It was

◄ The River Wye and the old quayside at Brockweir

long used for both coppicing and as wood pasture for grazing animals. However, in the 19th century the common was gradually occupied by squatters who built small cottages and enclosed the land in small fields. It is this pattern of settlement which is still visible today and accounts for many of the winding paths and lanes.

At the first lane, dog-leg right, then left and 250m further on, at a second lane, turn right and head round the left bend to pick up a sign for Offa's Dyke Path (ODP) which is now followed for the next 1.5km and soon turns right off the lane up over the brow of St Briavels Common. The route now descends over two fields in a northwesterly direction and turns right along the lane for 200m. At this point, look out for the waymark indicating a left turn off the lane and onto a byway.

Proceed along the byway for 350m and, at the end of the field on the left, turn left off ODP. Take the byway downhill, ignoring paths off right. The wide path descends round to the left through woodland, flanked initially by drystone walls, and soon turns right down zigzags to a crosspaths just before a house. Here turn left downhill, a little steeply at first, and then bear further round to the left, still heading down through the woodland.

Soon the River Wye can be glimpsed on the right through the trees. The path

emerges from the woods by the river just below Coed Ithel weir, which marks the limit of the tidal stream. Now turn left and follow the pleasant riverside path downstream. Just before reaching Brockweir Bridge you pass the old quayside, where the boats known as Severn Trows docked, having navigated the waters from Chepstow, in order to have their goods transferred into shallower barges for the onward journey.

The Devil's Pulpit from Brockweir

Distance 7km **Time** 2 hours 30
Terrain lanes, fields and wooded slopes;
with 200m of ascent **Map** OS Explorer
OL14 **Access** bus (69) from Monmouth
and Chepstow stops on the A466
opposite Brockweir

**Forget the direct route from Tintern – it's
a devil of a path – and follow the lie of the
land to reach one of the iconic
viewpoints in the lower Wye Valley.**

The Devil's Pulpit is rightly one of the
most visited natural attractions in the
lower Wye Valley. The most direct and
popular route crosses the river at Tintern
and climbs the steep slope which lower
down the valley forms the rocky outcrop
of Shorn Cliff, the haunt of climbers and
nesting birds. A start from Brockweir
allows a more leisurely ascent and also

the chance to see a well-preserved section
of Offa's Dyke. Brockweir is now a quiet
riverside village, worth exploring in its
own right.

Take the lane by the Malt House and the
14th-century Monks Hall towards the
Horse and Pony Protection Association
(HAPPA) centre. Opening times are
seasonal and there is a café. Turn left onto
the route of Offa's Dyke Path (ODP) uphill
above a small valley, bearing round to the
south and ignoring the route off left to
Madgett Hill. Cross a stile into a field and
bear slightly right, keeping to the line of
ODP up to and through a strip of
woodland and the dyke itself.

This makes a good spot to pause and
take in the view – to the west is the high
ground of the Trellech plateau with

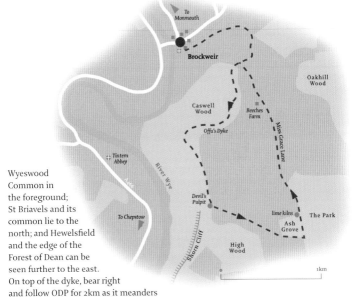

Wyeswood Common in the foreground; St Briavels and its common lie to the north; and Hewelsfield and the edge of the Forest of Dean can be seen further to the east. On top of the dyke, bear right and follow ODP for 2km as it meanders south and west up through woods along the line of the dyke itself. Pass a metal kissing gate on the left and shortly beyond reach the Devil's Pulpit rock with its famous view down to Tintern Abbey.

In one version of the famous story, the Devil gave up haranguing the Cistercians below to abandon their devotional life and descended from his airy rock to the abbey itself, suggesting he preach a sermon to them from a more conventional pulpit. The monks agreed but Old Nick was outwitted inside when he was showered with holy water, which sent him off towards Llandogo with his tail firmly between his legs.

Retrace steps to the metal kissing gate and turn right through it, off ODP, and across four fields with views opening out over the Severn Estuary (follow the hedge on the left in the first field, go diagonally right across the second and third to the corner of a wood, and keep the wood on the left in the fourth) to reach Miss Grace Lane. Turn left along the lane for 1.5km, passing old lime kilns on the left after 300m, to Beeches Farm. Pass to the right of the farm buildings across the lawn of the campsite. Now descend northwest over three fields to reach the outward route on Offa's Dyke Path once again and retrace steps downhill for 1km to Brockweir.

◀ Above Brockweir looking north to St Briavels Common

57

The Eagle's Nest and Tintern

Distance 1.5km (or 8km) **Time** 1 hour (or 3 hours) **Terrain** woodland, fields and lanes, with some steep paths and cliff edges **Map** OS Explorer OL14 **Access** bus (69) from Monmouth and Chepstow stops just east of Lower Wyndcliff car park

Take in the best viewpoint in the Wye Valley with an option to extend the walk and follow in the footsteps of the medieval monks of Tintern.

The Eagle's Nest viewpoint was created in 1828 for the Duke of Beaufort as part of the Piercefield Park Picturesque Walks, designed in the 18th century by Valentine Morris the Younger, with the 365 Steps as the culmination of the walk. Lower Wyndcliff car park on the A466 between Tintern and St Arvans has plenty of parking, some picnic tables and a useful information board.

Take the path (SP 365 Steps) across the road from the car park into woodland dominated by yew and beech. In 100m bear right in front of a small limestone cliff and soon start the 100m ascent of the Wyndcliff on a meandering path up rough steps, with views out over the Wye Gorge and beyond to the Severn Estuary. Near the top, as the path levels out, turn right at a junction onto the Wye Valley Walk path and in 150m come to the Eagle's Nest viewpoint down on the right.

For the shorter route return back down the Wye Valley Walk to Upper Wyndcliff car park and then left down through woodland to the start. For the longer option to Tintern, head northwards on

◂ The ruins of Tintern Abbey

the Wye Valley Walk for 1.5km along the top of Black Cliff Wood to the prominent earthworks of a hill fort. Here, the path descends steeply on the right. Below the fort, bear right for 100m, then left down to a stile. Here, leave the Wye Valley Walk and bear right (northeast) down three fields, past Reddings Farm on the right. At the far corner of the third field go through a gate, then immediately left over a stile into woodland, past an old quarry on the left, to a sunken track which leads down to Tintern with its abbey, shops and eateries.

To continue, retrace steps uphill, south along the Wye Valley Walk, past the left turn to Reddings Farm. This is the old medieval route from Tintern to St Arvans – the modern road along the valley was only built in 1824 – and perhaps still gives a hint of the seclusion the Cistercians originally sought in siting their abbey at Tintern. Look out for small tufa beds in the stream on the left as the way climbs to Penterry Lane (ignore the Wye Valley Walk's left turn across the stream). As the route levels out, it is prone to be overgrown – look out for a sturdy stick for some nettle-bashing or in high summer be prepared to escape right on the right of way which heads west to Penterry Lane.

At the lane, bear left and in 400m again turn left, up the driveway to Porthcasseg, whose name means 'mare's gate' and

recalls its former role as a staging post for horses. Pass to the rear of the buildings and follow the path to the right between barns onto a field-track heading south. Pass over the brow of the hill and descend past some old lime kilns on the left to Upper Wyndcliff car park, with views ahead to the Severn Estuary. At the rear of the car park, take the path on the right down through the woods, bearing left at the bottom of the slope to arrive at the small limestone cliff just up from the A466. Here, turn right down to the road and the start.

Chepstow Castle to Piercefield

Distance 6km Time 2 hours Terrain woods and parkland Map OS Explorer OL14 Access bus (69, 65) from Monmouth

From the imposing presence of one of the most magnificent castles in Wales, wander through the 'sublime' landscape of Piercefield Park.

From the mid-18th century, Piercefield Park just north of Chepstow became one of the most sought-after places for those wishing to indulge in the celebration of dramatic landscape scenery. For those embarking on a Wye Tour from Ross, it came to represent the culmination of their journey down the river. The estate was purchased by Valentine Morris and then landscaped by his son, also called Valentine. He created a series of 'sublime' walks along the cliffs, punctuated with features and viewpoints, exploiting the natural topography to its greatest effect.

Start by Chepstow Castle, where there is a car park, and take the surfaced path up Castle Dell past the stone from Plynlimon, which marks the start of the Wye Valley Walk, whose route is followed for the first half of the walk. The castle itself is in a magnificent state of preservation and its towers and walls remain an impressive monument to the Normans who sited this first stone castle in Wales on the last rocky spur of the Wye before it reaches the Severn. The corner tower nearest the car park is Marten's Tower, so named after the regicide Henry Marten, who was imprisoned here by Charles II for 20 years.

At the road, turn right and walk up the hill for 500m to where the route turns right, just before the leisure centre and the comprehensive school. At the rear of the car park, take the path into woodland and pass to the rear of the buildings. In 300m, go through a gap in the boundary wall and turn right down steps a short distance to

◄ Chepstow Castle

the Alcove viewpoint. This is the first of Morris' landscape features and gives a good view downstream to the castle.

Now bear left and follow the route northeastwards through Pierce Wood, past the now overgrown Platform whose view is now obscured. In just over 500m, the path swings left and then right to cross a dell before zigzagging up through the earthworks of an old hill fort to a now dilapidated grotto on its east side. Beyond the fort, follow the path round to the left and descend gently for 200m to a fork. Here bear left uphill, off the Wye Valley Walk, and soon cross over a stile into Piercefield Park, where the sad remains of Piercefield House stand on the right.

There are many stories associated with the house. Some say its owner is always ill-starred and it's true that Valentine Morris ended his days in poverty and that the second owner, George Smith, spent so much on the place that he bankrupted himself. Others point to American soldiers stationed here in World War II as just one case in its long decline, though their using the house for target practice is perhaps one of those apocryphal wartime stories. Far more engaging is the Spectre of the Mare's Pool, which used to stand by the west wall of the estate. From here on moonlit nights, it is said, a ghostly woman rises from the water on the back of a white horse and wings her way

northwards over the grounds, always in the direction of Porthcasseg, the Mare's Gate. Quite who this woman is or was or why she travels north is lost to time.

The onward route, however, leads from the house across the parkland to the edge of the racecourse and onto a track which heads south. Pass into the woodland and, after 400m, bear left along the high boundary wall which soon reaches the B4293 above Chepstow. Turn left and once again pass the entrance to the leisure centre and school. From here, retrace steps downhill to the start.

61

The cliffs of Lancaut

Distance **7km** Time **2 hours 30**
Terrain **lanes, field paths and some
steeper sections in Lancaut woods**
Map **OS Explorer OL14** Access **bus (69, 65)
from Monmouth**

**Experience riverside walking at its best
below and above the sheer limestone
cliffs of Lancaut.**

   Chepstow is a border town sited on a
bend in the River Wye, just above its
confluence with the Severn. The town
itself is full of historic buildings and since
well before the Normans arrived was
known as an important crossing point
between England and Wales.

   The route of the walk passes below and
above sheer cliffs used by climbers and the
river is tidal with mudflats. There is also
one short section of boulder scree to cross.

   From Chepstow Castle, walk past the

tourist information centre and Chepstow
Museum and down to the bridge over the
River Wye. This is known as the Old Wye
Bridge. Made of cast iron at the start of the
19th century, it was a replacement for a
series of timber bridges dating back to
medieval times. It gives good views back
upstream to the castle and down to the
modern road and rail bridges, beyond which
are the old wharves of the former port.

   On the far side of the bridge, take the
lane ahead uphill (SP Gloucestershire
Way). This is soon joined by Offa's Dyke
Path (ODP) from the right, which is now
followed northwards. Cross over the B4228
and, in another 150m, ODP bears left into a
field beside houses and up between an old
look-out tower and Chapelhouse Wood, so
named because of the site of a medieval
chantry chapel. At the far end of the field,
bear right along a large wall, then dog-leg

◀ Ruins of St James'
Church at Lancaut

left and right between the
houses before turning left
across a field to reach Lancaut
Nature Reserve. Here, leave
ODP and bear left into the
reserve. The path descends
through woodland, with the
Wye down on the left and
sheer limestone cliffs to
the right, from which
you are likely to hear
the calls of climbers
as they test their nerve
on routes that range
from the moderate
to the extreme.

As the path comes
near to the river, there is
a short section of boulder
scree to cross – for the exact route across,
follow the yellow markers and polished
rocks. Continue on the riverside path and
in another 500m, just before the river
bend, pass below Wintour's Leap. The
Royalist Sir John Wintour is well-known
for his horse's heroic pluck at the time of
the Civil War in launching itself down
these steep cliffs in order to escape the
pursuing Roundheads. Needless to say,
Sir John had not endeared himself to the
inhabitants of the Forest of Dean – it is
said that he had felled all but 200 of the
Dean's trees and ensured the forest was
staunchly Parliamentarian. Whatever the
truth, the impressive cliffs are no place
for horseplay.

Round the
bend, past the
disused Lancaut
quarry, is the ruin
of St James'
Church, once a
refuge for lepers.
Despite the
proximity of
Chepstow, the
high cliffs of
Wintour's Leap and
the Apostles Rocks on
the Piercefield
peninsula opposite still
make this a secluded spot.
At the church, bear right
uphill past a bench and over a
metal stile to a path junction just
short of some old lime kilns. Bear right
past the kilns and up to Lancaut Lane.
Here, a right turn brings you past the open
field of Spital Meend, an Iron Age fort, and
just beyond the first house on the right
Offa's Dyke itself crosses the lane.

Descend to the road junction and turn
right, round the bend, and 150m beyond
turn right onto Offa's Dyke Path once
more, which follows a line behind the
houses along the top of the cliffs. In
500m, the path reaches the road again and
bears right, round the bend, before
turning off right once more along a
walled garden to the entrance to Lancaut
Nature Reserve. From here, retrace the
outward route.

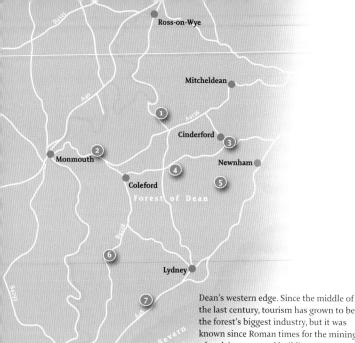

Dean's western edge. Since the middle of the last century, tourism has grown to be the forest's biggest industry, but it was known since Roman times for the mining of coal, iron ore, and building stone. Over the centuries the need for timber has significantly influenced the number and type of trees grown, from the oaks supplied to royal dockyards since the time of Elizabeth I to the modern plantations of quick-growing conifers favoured in the 20th century. Now, however, the area is undergoing a period of regeneration. The last of the collieries closed in 1965, the Forestry Commission is starting to restore plantations to mixed woodland, and many of the former industrial sites are being sensitively managed for the mutual benefit of residents, visitors and wildlife.

The Royal Forest of Dean is a triangular plateau of woodlands and commons lying between the Severn and Wye Valleys, and in 1938 it was designated England's first National Forest Park, with the towns of Coleford and Cinderford to the north, Lydney and Chepstow in the south, and the ancient administrative centre of St Briavels, now a charming village, on the

The Round House on the Kymin ▶

The Forest of Dean

Lydbrook and Sallowvallets

Distance 7km **Time** 2 hours **Terrain** forest
tracks and paths **Map** OS Explorer OL14
Access bus (35) from Ross or Monmouth

**Step back into the Forest of Dean's
industrial past and meander along
former railway tracks and through
woodland plantations.**

Lydbrook was one of the major
industrial centres of the Forest of Dean.
Coal from the nearby mines was brought
down to the lower end of the town to be
loaded onto barges for onward
transportation by barge to Hereford. With
the arrival of the railways in the mid 1800s
the Severn and Wye Line superseded the
river trade and ensured the mining
industry continued to flourish for another
century. Now tourism has replaced the
trains and many of the tracks have been
converted for the use of walkers and
cyclists. In Lydbrook the Jovial Colliers
pub is one of a number of reminders of
the area's past. Opposite, set into the

imposing wall is a plaque which
commemorates the removal by volunteers
of the huge coal heap that used to cover
what is now the recreation area, where
parking is available. Such was the amount
of slag dumped here over the decades that
it was known as the Blue Mound and
must have dominated the entire town.

From here, walk up Church Road and
take the first road on the right at the bend,
then follow the path on the left up past
the churchyard to a gate. Turn right onto
the disused railway line and follow it for
1.5km, passing above the spring to
Greathough Brook. Just beyond Horton
Bridge, at a fork, bear right uphill away
from the railway, which soon enters
Mirystock Tunnel, on a path which zigzags
up to the A4136. Cross the road and take
the path on the opposite side which soon
descends gently to meet the line of the
railway again on the far side of the tunnel,
with Mirystock Bridge a little beyond.
Continue for another 1km and, just

◀ Old railway line at Mirystock Bridge

*Map labels:*
To Keme Bridge and Ross
Lower Lydbrook
Upper Lydbrook
Hangerbury Inclosure
Forest of Dean
Mirystock Tunnel
Mirystock Bridge
Sallowvallets Inclosure
To Monmouth
Ropehouse Ditch
Speculation
0   1km

before the main cycle track is joined, turn right, down through Speculation car park, to the road beyond. This is one of a number of former colliery sites which have been given over to the tourist industry – its name perhaps recalls the precarious nature of mining in this area. From here, dog-leg right for 50m, then left across the road on the Wysis Way into woodland. The route follows a rising path westwards alongside Ropehouse Ditch into Sallowvallets Inclosure. Cross over a forestry track and continue along the ditch, whose stream here has been channelled with stone blocks. There are many enclosures in the forest, but Sallowvallets lays claim to being the first place in the area where conifers were planted. The original Weymouth pines, planted in 1781, are long since felled and conservation is now favouring mixed woodland, thereby restoring many areas to the condition envisaged by the 1688 Dean Reafforestation Act.

The Wysis Way now loops north across Ropehouse Ditch and back south before doubling north again for 400m to cross Ropehouse Ditch once more at a crosspaths. Here, turn left for 200m, with the ditch on the left, before bearing to the right and climbing more steeply to a track junction. Turn left round the bend for 250m, where the Wysis Way turns right off the track and almost immediately forks left onto a path, up through a dense conifer plantation for 200m to emerge onto the A4136 again.

Cross the road and, leaving the Wysis Way, dog-leg right and then left down the first lane on the left. Follow the lane for 300m and, just before the brow, bear right onto a woodland path along the western edge of Hangerbury Inclosure. In 250m, the path turns right onto a track between the woodland and fields, heading NNE over Hangerbury Hill with good views west. The path soon descends through woodland and, in another 500m, reaches a lane and the houses above Lydbrook. Cross over the lane and descend between houses, zigzagging more to the right than the left to reach Uphill Road, which brings you back down into Lydbrook a little below the start.

The Kymin and the Buckstone

Distance 8km **Time** 3 hours
Terrain undulating ground through
woodland and over fields, with 300m of
ascent **Map** OS Explorer OL14 **Access** bus
(35) from Monmouth to Staunton

**Take in the views on a real rollercoaster of
a walk on the edge of the Forest of Dean.**

The village of Staunton is perched high
up on the western edge of the Forest of
Dean and for centuries was on one of the
main routes into Wales. It still has an
impressive church and a welcoming pub,
the White Horse, where parking is
available with permission.

At the western edge of the village, take
the Restricted Byway northwards.
Descend left past St John the Baptist's
Well, which now seems rather out of place
all on its own. However, a chapel
dedicated to St John is recorded in the
14th century, though no trace of it has
been found. From here, pick a path
straight down the slope through the
beech and oak woodland to the forestry
track lower down. Turn left uphill onto

the route of the Wysis Way (WW), turning
right after 250m. The track descends
through deciduous woodland to a fork
junction. Here, take the left track uphill
and look out for a WW sign up left to
cross the busy Staunton Road.

Continue on the WW, but after 300m
ignore the next WW sign pointing left
across fields and continue into Beaulieu
Wood. This woodland was acquired by the
Woodland Trust in 2001 – their intention
is to restore the mixed broadleaf trees
which existed before the area was planted
with conifers in the 1950s and which first
attracted the Kymin Club, a wealthy group
of friends, at the turn of the 19th century
to landscape what was then known as
Beaulieu Grove with paths and viewing
points. After the next left-hand bend, at a
slanted crosspaths, turn sharp left uphill.

The path soon bears round to the right
on a rising traverse up to outcrops of
moss-covered stone, and twists through
the outcrops to emerge onto a wooded
ridge. Follow the path along the ridge,
past a viewpoint on the right, to shortly

◄ At the Buckstone looking west

arrive at the Kymin. The top of the hill is dominated by the Round House and the Naval Temple. Nelson had breakfast here in 1802, but it is not recorded whether he enjoyed the magnificent view, which allegedly takes in 10 counties, though he apparently grumbled that the Dean was not planting nearly enough of his 'oaks' to supply the navy. The name of the hill appears to be a corruption of *cae maen*, Welsh for 'stone field', though these have clearly been removed from the lush lawn nearby which is ideal for a picnic or a snooze.

To continue, descend past the Naval Temple and car park to where the Offa's Dyke Path takes you through a metal kissing gate signed for Redbrook. At first, the well-signed path passes through woods and then down across fields, with views of the Wye Valley and Forest of Dean, before joining Duffield's Lane. A little past Duffield's Farm, you come to the line of the former Coleford to Monmouth railway. Here, where the track bends right, take the left fork on a small path, just before a cottage, and descend to the road with a mill pond beyond.

Turn left onto the road and, just after the right bend, take the footpath rising left up to a stile. Here, recross the dismantled railway and bear right uphill, steeply at first, through the woodland of Knockalls Inclosure. At the third forestry

track turn left and in 200m bear right past Knockalls Lodge, originally inhabited by a single woodsman who had responsibility for managing the forestry. Round the bend, take the left fork beside a drystone wall up to the dwellings of Buckstone on Staunton Meend.

Pass to the right of the houses, climbing beside a drystone wall to reach the triangulation point through a gate, with the Buckstone itself just to the left. It used to be a logan, but in 1885 a group of travelling actors rocked it off its base and it crashed down the hillside. Somehow it was restored to its original place and, secured by iron and cement, it no longer rocks, though it provides good clambering. To descend to Staunton, continue along the path beside the wall down through the woods.

Welshbury Fort and the Dobunni's last stand

Distance 3km **Time** 1 hour
Terrain woodland tracks and paths
Map OS Explorer OL14 **Access** bus (30, 31)
from Coleford to Littledean, near
Cinderford; to reach the start, walk for
1km northwards up George Lane

**Discover the hidden hill fort of
Welshbury, tucked away in woodland on
the eastern fringe of the Forest of Dean –
an ideal outing for marauding children.**

Welshbury hill fort is thought to date
from the Iron Age – a Celtic coin and a
Roman spearhead have been found here –
and the site's occupation may well stretch
back to Neolithic times. It is also
reputedly the fort where the Dobunni
tribe fought their last battle against the
Romans. Its detailed history, however, is
still shrouded in doubt as the site has
never been systematically excavated.

What is clear is the system of ditches and
ramparts – there is a triple line on the
south and west side and a single one on
the steeper north and east slopes. Recent
use of lidar (radar with lasers) has given a
clearer picture, but the hill still hides its
secret past.

There is a straightforward approach
from the layby at the edge of the Forestry
Commission land (GR672146) 1km north
of Littledean along George Lane, where
there is space for a few cars. From here,
walk northeastwards into woodland up a
track, passing houses set back on the
right, and along the top of Chestnuts
Inclosure. In another 200m, where a track
comes in from the right, continue ahead
and soon arrive at the northern edge of
the woodland. Pass through the gate and
cross the clearing to the southern edge of
Welshbury Wood – there are good views

◂ Looking west from near Welshbury Wood

east and west from this spot. In the wood, bear left onto a path which heads uphill (avoid the track which follows the western edge of the wood) and in 250m pass through the outer ditches and ramparts of Welshbury Fort.

Continue a little further to the top of the hill, from where the extensive earthworks are clearly visible and can be explored, brambles permitting. The north side, in particular, is fearsomely steep for any attacker and though the whole site is now covered in trees it is still possible to gain an idea of just how commanding a position the fort occupies. Such is the sensitivity of the site that, in order to thin the trees without causing damage to what may lie just below ground level, the owners of the land, the Forestry Commission, have recently reverted to using horses for dragging out the felled timber.

To return, either retrace the outward route or continue a little further to the northern edge of the fort and then bear westwards on a faint path, which initially follows the top of the fortifications, before descending more steeply down the western side of the fort through the series of ramparts and ditches themselves. On reaching the track lower down, turn left and proceed gently uphill to return to the southern edge of the wood and the outward route.

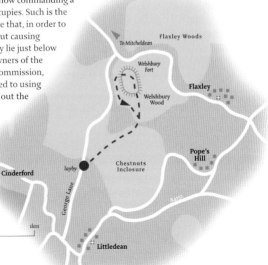

Flaxley Woods

To Mitcheldean

Welshbury Fort

Flaxley

Welshbury Wood

Cinderford

layby

George Lane

Chestnuts Inclosure

Pope's Hill

0   1km

Littledean

Speech House loop

Distance **6km** Time **2 hours**
Terrain **woodland paths and tracks**
Map **OS Explorer OL14** Access **bus (30)
from Cinderford to Beechenhurst Lodge**

**Explore the heart of the Forest of
Dean and popular Cannop Ponds,
before wandering back through
Russell's Inclosure.**

Beechenhurst Lodge is found right in
the centre of the Forest of Dean. It is the
former site of Speech House Colliery,
though little evidence of the industry
remains as the area has been developed
for tourists. It makes a good base for a
whole day with the family or as a place
simply to park before heading off deep
into the forest. It can be a popular place in
high season, but you don't have to go far
to lose the crowds by the café and
adventure playground. There are a

number of marked routes, including a
Sculpture Trail to the rear of the lodge.
This walk covers the ground to the south.

Start at the far lower corner of the car
park at a gate onto a cycle track heading
northwest (SP Cycle Trail). A left turn after
30m, down through the woodland, brings
you to the main cycle trail. Here, turn left
(SP Cannop Wharf) and follow the trail to
the road (B4226). Cross straight over and
50m after the trail joins the road to Cannop
car park, opposite a gate, bear right onto a
woodland path which runs parallel to the
road. This trail makes for pleasant walking
and soon reaches the first of the ponds at
Cannop and a picnic site. The ponds were
formed in 1827 by the damming of the
stream that runs through the Cannop
Valley. The intention was that they would
provide power for the iron furnaces that
were then in use at Parkend. The scheme

◄ Cannop Ponds

was not a commercial success and the ponds were given over to birds and other wildlife.

Pass through the car park and at the rear, just beyond the gate on the cycle trail, again bear right to a path on the edge of the pond (or stay on the cycle trail if you prefer). At the far end of the second pond, rejoin the cycle trail at a five-way junction. Here, take the Gloucestershire Way Path (GWP) sharp left through a gate heading northeast up into the woodland of Russell's Inclosure. In 500m, arrive at a crosspaths and turn left. Now head north for 600m and, beyond a dip, turn right (east) to climb between an older plantation on the left and a newer one on the right on a broad track. As the track levels out, reach a junction and turn left (north) across level ground with forestry on the left and cleared ground on the right. After 400m, at a fork, bear left into woodland and soon descend for 500m, muddy in places, to cross a stile and fence. Now turn right (northeast) and follow a path through open woodland, passing the 'Mahony' beech tree to the Speech House.

This building, now a hotel, and the stone cross on the opposite side of the road mark the traditional centre of the Forest of Dean. The Speech Court is still held here, presided over by the Forest

Verderers whose role is to look after the venison (wild animals) and the vert (shelters). Today the power of the Verderers is much reduced since the time of Charles II when the Speech House was built, though the position is still held for life.

From the cross, continue on the GWP for 50m and then, leaving the route, turn left (southwest) through a gate. Now follow the clear path through woodland, staying roughly parallel to the road down to the buildings at Beechenhurst.

Soudley Bridge and the Old Dean Road

Distance 2.5km **Time** 45 mins
Terrain woodland paths and lanes
Map OS Explorer OL14 **Access** bus (717)
from Cinderford or Lydney stops in
Soudley, at the White Horse Inn at the
top of Lower Road

**This route is ideal for those wanting a
walk which is quick but full of history
in the charming surroundings of a
wooded valley.**

The village of Soudley is tucked away
between the towns of Cinderford and
Lydney. Most visitors come to see the
Dean Heritage Centre and the Ponds but
there is good walking to the south from
Soudley Bridge.

At the bottom of Lower Road in Soudley
is the old bridge over Soudley Brook by
the recreation area, where parking is
available. Take the signed Forest Footpath
at the rear of the parking area southwest
into woodland with Soudley Brook on the
right. The path soon bears left away from
the brook and heads uphill along the line
of what is thought to be a Roman road.
There is some doubt as to the exact line
of the route the Romans would have
taken from Lydney northwards to
Ariconium, near the modern town of
Ross. However, it is likely that the old
Dean Road, which may have predated the
Romans, keeps to much the same line.
Whatever the origins of the route, some
stone surfacing and kerbing can be seen
along the path.

After 500m, you reach a modern forest
road. Here, bear left along the verge for
100m before turning left along another
forest road towards Bradley Hill. In 300m,
you come to the edge of the woodland
and a clearing dotted with houses.

◂ Leaf fall in woods on Bradley Hill

Continue ahead uphill for 150m to the top of the rise and into woodland again. The woodland in this area is well worth visiting in springtime for the covering of bluebells.

At the track junction, turn left and head north with views back over Soudley. The track soon descends gently to join the lane on its left before passing through a barrier, where it becomes a fenced path and starts to descend the ridge with a small ravine on the left and old quarry workings to the right. These can be explored by climbing over a stile. A little further on, at a path junction, take the right fork down through the woodland. At the bottom of the slope, bear round to the left, passing above Dean Heritage Centre and in 250m cross an old packhorse stone footbridge over Soudley Brook. At this point, the Dean Heritage Centre can be reached on a path to the right alongside the brook.

From the bridge, continue ahead to emerge onto Tramway Road. In the early 19th century, horse-drawn tramroads were developed in the Forest of Dean to transport coal and ironstone to local ironworks. This tramroad linked the area, via a tunnel through Bradley Hill, to the River Severn at Bullo, to the east, and Lydney, to the south. Now turn left and follow the lane downhill to another bridge over the brook. Just after the bridge, turn right onto a pleasant grassy path which leads back beside the brook to Soudley Bridge itself.

St Briavels and the Slade Brook

Distance **5km** Time **1 hour 30**
Terrain **lanes, fields and woodland**
Map **OS Explorer OL14** Access **limited
bus service (705) from Monmouth and
(707) Chepstow**

**Enjoy the sense of history and nature on
this short walk from the Dean's most
famous village.**

St Briavels is today one of the best
known villages in the area. It stands high
up above the Wye Valley and its
commanding position echoes its
importance as the one time
administrative and judicial centre of the

Forest of Dean. The Norman castle and
church dominate the village centre and
exude a great sense of history. You can
even stay in the castle – it has been a
youth hostel for over 50 years – though in
former times a visit was not so sought
after. You could be arraigned before the
Court of Mine Law, had you usurped the
privileges of the Free Miners who claimed
the sole right to mine in the Dean, and if
found guilty you might even have been
thrown in the dungeon. The village itself
was famous for its quarrels – though in
the form of bolts for crossbows.

From the castle, walk down Mork Road
past the church and in 400m, at the
hairpin bend, bear right down Mork Lane.
This follows the line of the medieval road

northwards to Redbrook and gives good views over the valley ahead. Descend, steeply at times, to the ford through the Slade Brook and on to the road beyond – the house to the left under which the brook flows is Sladbrook, a fine early 19th-century former mill, and across the road are the gables and mullioned windows of Mork Farm, which date back to the early 17th century.

Here, turn right along the road and just beyond the bend take the footpath right through a gate into a strip of woodland back towards the Slade Brook. The alder-lined brook takes you eastwards over fields into woodland. Here, in the brook's streambed, begins a spectacular if easily-missed series of tufa dams, one of the longest in Britain. This remarkable rock is formed when limestone dissolved in water is deposited on rocks and debris.

At a footbridge in the woodland, cross to the other bank and a little way up, where the path gives out, recross to the original side, picking a path through the trees to reach a forestry track which crosses the brook where a side stream joins.

Now follow the broad track to the right of the brook as it climbs uphill and leaves the woodland to reach Bearse Farm, which

stands in an area inhabited by humans since Neolithic times – one of the finest examples of a polished flint axe was found near here.

Just before the farm, take the footpath on the right which rises between horse paddocks. Beyond, enter woodland and bear left across a dip. Leave the woodland and go uphill towards Bushyard Barn, passing to the right. Now aim for the far right corner of this long field, with the tower of St Briavels Church away on the left. Head across the next two fields, following the fence on the left and, where the fence turns sharp left towards the church tower, bear left across the field to a gate and stile in the wall opposite. Here, cross onto Mork Road once more and turn left back up the hill to St Briavels.

◀ St Briavels Castle

Woolaston Ridge and Severn views

Distance 8km Time **2 hour 30**
Terrain **fields and woodland**
Map **OS Explorer OL14** Access **bus (73) from Chepstow stops at Woolaston Church Lane**

From near the banks of the Severn, traverse ancient lanes and fields up onto the southern slopes of the Forest of Dean.

The walk starts south of Woolaston village at the layby on the north side of the A48 (GR589992), where there is a parking area and toilets. Turn left onto the road at the rear of the layby and left again along the lane to the church of St Andrew. This impressive building stands at some distance to the southwest of where the modern village has grown up, but it is thought that the site is actually close to the line of the Roman road that runs from Gloucester to Caerleon. At this

point, it passed just to the north of the church before joining the modern line of the A48 just above Stroat, whose name may be a corruption of 'Street'.

At the rear of the churchyard, go through a gate and pass to the right of the farm buildings into a small field. At the far end, turn left onto a green lane which leads to a footbridge over Black Brook and into a field – this could well be the line of the Roman road. Where the hedge bends left bear right through a gateway and down to a lane, formerly known as Millin Lane, which leads right uphill to High Woolaston Farm.

At the bend, turn left past farm buildings and then right along a short walled track to fields. With Piccadilly Brook to the left, make for the woodland in the top left corner of the second field. Here reputedly stands the tallest poplar tree in the Forest of Dean. Cross a stile

◄ Stone barn at High
  Woolaston Farm

into chestnut woodland
and turn left on a small
path through Ashwell
Grove, which soon
leads up to a
forestry track. Here,
bear right uphill for
500m before turning
left onto the
Gloucestershire Way (GW).

Follow the route out of the
woodland, across a lane and
along the bottom edge of a
field, with good views to the
south. To the north is an area
called Poor's Allotment, a reminder that
this was once open common, used for
essential grazing and coppicing. Go
through a small copse and onto a lane
and, after 400m where the lane bends
back left, leave the GW and take a path left
down through ancient coppiced
woodland. This is known as Ridley
Bottom and is now a nature reserve
managed by Gloucestershire Wildlife
Trust. In 200m, where the woodland ends,
cross a stile, on the right, and head for the
top of the sloping field to the pool of
Slade Well. Cross the stile 50m beyond
and bear right in a southerly direction to
the bottom corner of the field and onto
Rosemary Lane.

Go left for 150m and just after the left
bend take the path left down fields to
Stroat, dog-legging left, then right after
the first field to pick up a stream down to

the A48 main road. It is thought that this
path follows the line of a prehistoric
trackway, which continues all the way
down to the Severn, where a stone slab
called the Broad Stone marks an ancient
crossing point.

At the road, turn left and then left
again through the buildings of Stroat
Farm, bearing right up to a field gate.
The final section of the walk follows the
line of an old lane that was still in use in
the 18th century, but has now been largely
lost beneath the plough. Go diagonally
right up this field and along the top of the
next one onto the lane past Ashwell
Grange. Now head down and up fields,
across two streams (the second one is
Piccadilly Brook), in a NNE direction to
reach High Woolaston Farm once more.
From here the outward route will take
you back to the start.

Rising steeply from Monmouth to the village of Trellech, this upland area stretches all the way to Chepstow. From its plateau, there are striking views westwards across the Usk Valley towards the Black Mountains. On the eastern side steep slopes and gushing streams plunge down into the Wye Gorge and were once sites for the industries of iron smelting, wire-working and paper production. Farmland and woodland, both ancient and modern, are criss-crossed by lanes and trackways, connecting a large number of hamlets and settlements, many of which date back to a Norman foundation. Indeed, the medieval village of Trellech was one of the most important towns in Wales. The plateau still retains a sense of seclusion and you can wander for miles in varied and tranquil surroundings.

Harold's Stones at Trellech ▶

The Trellech to Chepstow Plateau

The secluded slopes of Cwmcarfan

Distance 7km **Time** 2 hours 30
Terrain field paths, lanes and woodland
tracks; a steep climb up to the ridge
Map OS Explorer OL14 **Access** bus (65)
from Monmouth or Chepstow: the walk
can be joined halfway round on the B4293
at Five Trees bus stop

**Nestling below the ridge that runs along
to Trellech, this walk is full of delight,
and a great place for an evening stroll to
watch the sun set.**

Tucked away in the folds of the hills
which face west into Wales, there is a far
greater sense of remoteness at Cwmcarfan
than the distance of 6km from
Monmouth would suggest. Now there are
a few houses, some farms and the church
of St Cadog. This impressive building
stands on an intervening ridge, framed
above by the woods of the Trellech
plateau, from where a lane circuitously
wends its way. The easier approach is

from the old A40 road, just to the south
of Mitchel Troy, and as you climb away
from the valley there is a real sense of
entering a forgotten cirque of fields and
ridges, though at the end of the 19th
century over 200 people are recorded as
living in the parish.

From the church, where there is parking
for a few cars, walk back down the hill and
in 150m turn right on the track down
towards Church Farm. Across Cwmcarfan
Brook bear diagonally right up over two
fields and then round to the south, before
climbing up to the east of Cwmcarfan
Court to meet its driveway. Here, a right
turn onto the lane leads uphill for 1km to
the road junction with good views back
westwards. Just to the right can be seen the
settlement of Craig-y-dorth, reputedly the
site of Owain Glyndwr's defeat of Henry
IV's English forces in 1404 – they were
chased all the way down the far side of the
hill to the Monnow Gate at Monmouth.

◀ Field trees near Craig-y-dorth

Now bear right, passing the entrance to Caer Llan Study Centre, along the quiet lane up to the B4293. Cross this to follow the minor road towards Chapel Farm and at the bend, a little before the farm, take the field-path on the right down to the road again. Here, turn left along the grassy verge for 350m (the bus stops along here at Five Trees), taking the second footpath on the right along a private road into woodland. Pass the entrance to High Glanau and Glanau Lodge and 500m from the road, where the track bends right, continue ahead. Descend just beyond the gables of Glanau Cottages to a barrier, where there is an old boundary stone.

Here, fork right down across a stream and turn right onto a bridleway that leads through the mixed woodland. The path climbs a little and curves round to the left before descending southwest to join a forestry track. Bear right downhill on the track and, where the Forestry Commission land ends, keep ahead for 200m and then turn right down a field with a cottage on the left to reach the track beyond. Here, turn right onto the track and descend past stables. Now follow the pleasant country lane for another 1km back down to Cwmcarfan and enjoy the views westwards as the hills of the Black Mountains appear through the gaps in the hedges.

Beacon Hill from Trellech

Distance **4km** Time **1 hour 30**
Terrain **fields, lanes and tracks**
Map **OS Explorer OL14** Access **bus (65)**
from Monmouth and Chepstow

Be enchanted by this ancient village and the views from the nearby high ground of Beacon Hill.

Today Trellech is a vibrant village which boasts a church with a famous octagonal tower, a welcoming pub, the Lion Inn, and a primary school. In the 13th and 14th centuries it was one of the largest towns in Wales. However, the exact whereabouts of the medieval village is the subject of competing local theories. One locates it beneath current buildings surrounding the church and the former motte and bailey castle; another points to recent archaeological finds and surveys in fields a little to the south of the modern village centre, in the area around the Virtuous Well.

Opposite the church, a lane between the Babington Centre and the pub leads away from the village. At the left-hand bend take the signed footpath on the right across a field. Bear diagonally left and pass through a gap in the fence to join a tractor track on the field edge heading towards Upper Barn. In the field before the barn, cross into the field on the left and follow the waymarks up past the barn, bearing slightly left. Just beyond a brick stables, take the right fork up over fields to Beacon Road.

Here, a dog-leg right for 30m, then left onto a bridleway leads through woodland. After 100m, at a crosspaths, turn right onto a forest track and pass through a vehicle barrier. The track climbs a little and brings you out onto the cleared area near the broad top of Beacon Hill. The geology of this area is markedly different from much

◄ The Virtuous Well at Trellech

of the lower Wye Valley – the peaty soil is dotted with white stones which hint at the quartz conglomerate rock underlying this heathy acidic podzol. It provides ideal growing conditions for a rare and local bramble, Rubus Trelleckensis, which is known on only a few sites in this part of the Wye Valley.

Continue a little beyond a cattle grid and take the first track right uphill. Pass through a gate and into woodland and soon arrive at Beacon Hill viewpoint, where there is a useful information board and a picnic table. The very top of the hill, marked by a triangulation point, is in the trees away to the left of the onward path. Now follow the path downhill through woodland to a

car park. Here, turn left along Beacon Road and then right at the junction. After 500m, look out for the sign on the right for the Virtuous Well.

Known also as St Anne's Well, it is a natural spring which was reputed from medieval times to have the power to heal a variety of ailments, such as scurvy and abdominal pains. If you are here on midsummer's eve keep an eye out for the fairies, which come to dance near the spring and drink its water from harebell cups. From here, cross the bridge and head left over fields on a waymarked path to the back of the village car park.

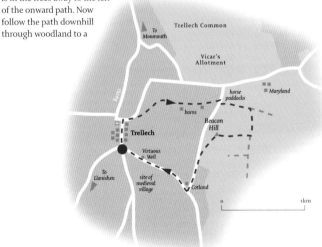

85

Trellech and Hygga

Distance **7km** Time **2 hours**
Terrain **field, woodland paths and lanes**
Map **OS Explorer OL14** Access **bus (65)
from Monmouth and Chepstow**

**From the medieval village of Trellech, on
the high ground between the Wye and
Usk valleys, this undulating route passes
a number of places of interest, including
some standing stones, a 17th century
furnace and an Iron Age hill fort.**

From the car park, follow signs to
Harold's Stones on the southern edge of
the village. One local legend has it that in
a contest with the Devil these stones were
hurled by Jack O'Kent, a huge giant, from
Ysgyryd Fawr (Skirrid Mountain), a hill over
16km to the northwest. Archaeologists
date their positioning from the Bronze
Age. At any rate, they gave the village its
name (*tre* – 'three', *llech* – 'stone').

From the stones, go along the road for

50m, away from the village, and at the
bend take the tree-lined path on the right
signed Penarth Brook & Llanishen. It
immediately crosses Penarth Brook and in
200m veers left and soon enters an open
field. Bear to the left downhill and in
200m, where a sidestream from the left
meets the brook, cross the stream and
head up the slope a little way before
bearing right uphill along a fence on the
right. At the top of the field between two
stiles take the permissive path into
Woolpitch Wood, signed Trellech Furnace.

Go downhill through the conifer
woodland and cross Penarth Brook once
more on a footbridge. Turn left to follow
the brook's right bank downhill, in 250m
passing the former site of Trellech Furnace
in a clearing – here from the 17th century
iron ore was smelted to make pig iron, the
nearby stream being used to power a
waterwheel which operated the bellows of
the furnace. After another 250m, where

a sidestream comes down from the right, cross the brook and follow the track uphill as the brook drops away on the right. As fields open out on the left, cross a stile into woodland and descend on a meandering path to a lane by a house.

Turn left and follow the sunken lane uphill, steeply at first, past Pant-glas House to the B4293 road. Cross over and take the lane and bridleway, signed Hygga and Parkhouse. The lane descends to Hygga with views left to Beacon Hill, ahead to St Briavels Common and right to the woods above Tintern. The buildings at Hygga date back to the 16th century (there are old barns and a restored dovecote visible) and the land was once worked by the monks of Tintern Abbey, Hygga being the site of a former manor house. This area is also the source of the Anghidi River which eventually plunges down to Tintern – its tree-lined course is visible to the southeast. Just beyond the farm is a huge hollow sycamore tree by a remarkable walled

walk-in drinking trough for horses.

The bridleway now descends and rises with a clear view left to a rounded hill, the site of an Iron Age hill fort, before descending again to a stream. Turn left and follow the stream for 100m, then go straight ahead, with the stream on the right, on a path signed Trelleck Cross, ignoring the bridleway as it turns right uphill. At the top of the field, cross a stile above the fenced-off Ffynnon Gaer ('Spring of the Fort') and follow the path across the field as it bears right uphill and becomes a sunken way which leads up to Trelleck Cross. At the lane, turn right and pass the base of an old cross just before the crossroads. Turn left along the lane for just over 500m and bear left again at a junction to reach Trellech.

◀ Mown hay near Pant-glas House

Wolvesnewton and Gaer Fawr

Distance **7km** Time **2 hours 30**
Terrain **fields and lanes; some steep
slopes** Map **OS Explorer OL14**
Access **no bus service**

**Enter the lair overlooked by one of
the largest, but least known, hill forts
in Gwent.**

Wolvesnewton is hidden among the
steep slopes and narrow lanes between
the high ground of the Trellech plateau
and the Usk Valley. The curious English
name stems from a local family called
Wolf, prominent in the 14th century,
rather than from the recollection of any
mythical pack of wild beasts. The origin of
the church dates from earlier still and its
dedication to St Thomas a Beckett firmly
links the area to the Normans. There are
no graves on the northern side of the
church and the medieval cross has been
converted into a war memorial. Now
sparsely populated, this cirque of ridges
must once have been thronging with busy
rural life. Indeed, the area's occupation
stretches back to the Iron Age and even
Neolithic times.

Take the lane westwards just in front of
the church and soon pass between some
houses to fields beyond. Cross through
six fields in a westerly direction for 1km,
over the brow of the hill and down to
Nantygelli Farm. Gold is apparently still
to be found in the stream near here.
A former servant at the farm was
reputedly frightened out of his wits by a
ghostly apparition who ordered the poor
man to dispose of a purse containing 12
guineas in a nearby stream. This was to
prevent the ghost's wife from getting

Nantygelli
Farm

Wolvesnewton

□ barn

To B4293
and Devauden

Cae
Pwtto

hill
fort

■ model farm

**Gaer
fawr**

To Shirenewton

Newchurch

0   1km

hold of the small fortune. When the story got out people searched high and low, but in vain; the gold was never found.

Pass to the left of the farm and climb the field beyond to the road. Go over the crossroads up the single-track road, which leads steeply uphill for 750m where the earthworks to Gaer Fawr hill-fort can be seen on the right beyond Camp House. This hill-fort is one of the most extensive in this part of Wales and occupies a commanding position with steep slopes on all but the south side. It is thought there was a double rampart which met in the southeast corner and encircled the west side, with possibly a third outer ring lower down. The fort itself lies on private land, but an idea of its impressive size and

position can still be gained by walking along the lane.

Continue past the fort to a junction, turn left and, in 50m at a fork in the road, bear left again. Follow the road for a little over 1km to the outskirts of the ridge-top hamlet of Newchurch – it has a small church dedicated to St Peter, set on the ridge with good views of the surrounding countryside.

Take the path northwards 100m before the road junction in Newchurch, and wriggle your way down over six fields to Cae Pwtto Wood (in the first field follow the right-hand hedge, in the second left, bear left along the top of the third, in the fourth bear right down to the corner of a copse, and through the next two head northeast to a stile into the wood). The path meanders through the west side of the wood for 200m and then into a field to descend to a barn and a track: this leads up to Lower House Farm. Here, cross the road and climb the lane to return to Wolvesnewton Church.

◄ Above Wolvesnewton looking west to the Black Mountains

Devauden and Chepstow Park Wood

Distance **6km** Time **2 hours**
Terrain **woodland paths and lanes over
undulating ground** Map **OS Explorer OL14**
Access **bus (65) from Monmouth or
Chepstow**

**Step back into the haunts of
highwaymen before discovering the
hidden Fedw Valley.**

Chepstow Park Wood was once part of a
great swathe of woodland stretching in an
arc from Chepstow to Trellech and
Monmouth and up the Monnow Valley on
the Welsh side, and round to Ross,
through the current Forest of Dean, and
all the way to the Severn below
Gloucester. Over the centuries, the woods

have been enclosed for coppicing and
pasturing, and many, such as Chepstow
Park Wood, are now managed by the
Forestry Commission, who are gradually
restoring the plantations of the 20th
century to mixed woodland.

The walk starts at the village green in
Devauden, where John Wesley preached
his first sermon in Wales in October 1739
to a congregation numbering in the
hundreds. A path on the south side of the
green, to the right of the village hall, leads
into Chepstow Park Wood (SP Itton). After
250m, take the second path on the left
between conifer plantations and then in
another 300m, at a forestry track, dog-leg
left then right into mixed woodland to

continue in a southeasterly direction beside a tumbledown drystone wall on the right. Soon pass over a crosspaths (it is possible to detour right here for a few hundred metres to the site of some small earthworks) and in just over 500m, at a broad forestry track, turn left and almost immediately, at the fork, again bear left downhill, with deciduous woodland on the left, conifers away on the right and views ahead to Gaer Hill. In 500m, at a fork in the track, bear left to continue downhill to the road.

Cross over into the deciduous woodland of New Wood and descend northwards down a sunken lane to a crosstrack. Dog-leg left for 30m, then right to continue downhill to the houses and lanes of the hidden Fedw Valley. Here, you'll find a scattering of houses enclosed by the steep slopes of the valley, much of which is covered in conifer plantation, but the name Y Fedw means The Birches and hints at the older woods that used to cover the area. Many of the walled lanes were probably made by squatters who illegally settled here as woodsmen and workers at the nearby Tintern wireworks.

At the junction turn right and in 5m, at the bend, turn left up a sunken lane which soon curves round to the left and passes a house where it becomes a path between fields. Continue uphill for a little over 500m, with views across the Fedw Valley, until the path emerges onto a lane which leads back into Devauden.

St Arvans and Itton Court

Distance **7.5km** Time **2 hours**
Terrain **field paths and lanes**
Map **OS Explorer OL14** Access **bus (69)
from Monmouth and Chepstow**

**Follow the medieval route to one of
Tintern Abbey's granges before circling
the countryside surrounding Itton Court.**

St Arvans is easily bypassed on the road
north of Chepstow through the Wye
Valley. However, it pays to spend a little
time exploring the village. The walk starts
from the restored Victorian fountain at
the A466 junction. Walk through the
village and turn left up Church Lane to
the church of St Arvan which is worth
seeing, not least for its unusual octagonal
tower and its curious dormer windows.

Beyond the church, follow the lane
round the bend, then bear left onto a
fenced path that leads between the
recreation area and fields. Cross into the
field ahead through a lever-board stile

and down along the fence into a slight
dip. In the next field bear right and follow
a line of oak trees, which mark the line of
the old medieval way to Rogerstone
Grange, one of the most important
former granges of Tintern Abbey.
The field on the right, to the east of the
grange, used to be known as St John's
Mead and a number of limekilns were
purposely sited here, on what is a
geological faultline. The underlying rock
to the south of here is limestone, with
shale to the north which changes to old
red sandstone near the ridge.

At the grange, turn left along the track
for 50m, then right along a fenced path to
pass to the south of the buildings and into
the field beyond (the path has been
diverted from the route shown on the
map). Now follow the right-hand field-
hedge and in the second field bear right
through a gap and along the eastern edge
of Pilmoore Wood for 50m, before crossing

◀ Restored Victorian
fountain at St Arvans

a stile left into the wood: this is good for snowdrops and bluebells in spring, though it can be muddy underfoot, a sign that the underlying free-draining limestone has been left behind. The path now heads westwards up through the wood before crossing three more fields (in the second field bear right over a stile into the adjacent field) to descend to a track which bears left past houses down to a crossroads with the B4293.

Here, take the rising lane opposite, passing Itton Court after 500m, to Itton Church. Dedicated to St Deiniol, it sits close by the former manor house of Itton Court and was much restored in the 19th century. Look for the large squared blocks in the tower which are made from the local grey limestone and in the porch the coat of arms with the Latin motto *Gratus Si Amicus* – 'Welcome, if a friend'. Continue

beyond the church for 400m before turning left along another pleasant lane with good views back to Itton Court and in just over 1km reach the B4293 again at Howick Farm.

Set above the level of the road, the stone farmhouse gives the impression of great age – its origins date from the 16th century. Pass to the left of the farm buildings into the fields beyond and cross the first two in a northerly direction, heading for the mast on Gaer Hill. Then bear right (ENE) over the brow of the hill along three field edges, with views ahead to St Arvans, to the track which leads north to Rogerstone Grange. Here, dog-leg across this track and along the edge of the next field down into the dip. Bear left up the next field and reach the lever-board stile once again. From here, retrace the outward route back to St Arvans.

The stones of Gray Hill

Distance 3km **Time** 1 hour **Terrain** open slopes and forest tracks; the ascent of Gray Hill is steep **Map** OS Explorer OL14 **Access** no bus service

Climb one of the best natural viewpoints in South Wales and wander amongst ancient stones and woodland.

This route provides an ideal short walk to be combined with local sightseeing, or a leisurely stroll in good weather to make the best of the views. The walk starts at Foresters' Oaks car park and picnic site on the Usk road north of the village of Llanvair Discoed; it's above Wentwood Reservoir on the edge of Wentwood Forest. There are a number of picnic benches overlooking the reservoir.

It is salutary to think that until the early 19th century the Foresters' Oaks were in no way connected with recreation. It was here that the medieval Forest Courts were held and the great oaks themselves served a capital purpose for those unlucky enough to be caught poaching or stealing from the forest.

From the car park, bear right across the road up a surfaced track for 400m, past some houses where the path narrows. Beyond the houses leave the path, which contours the hill, and turn left through a gate onto Gray Hill Common, climbing steeply with views down to the reservoir and beyond to the Severn Estuary.

At the top, the panoramic views on a clear day are stunning and it is quite